ELDER LAW

2nd Edition

by
Margaret C. Jasper

Oceana's Legal Almanac Series
Law for the Layperson

2001
Oceana Publications, Inc.
Dobbs Ferry, New York

Library of Congress Control Number 2001132453

ISBN: 0-379-11354-6

Oceana's Legal Almanac Series: Law for the Layperson
ISSN 1075-7376

©2001 by Oceana Publications, Inc.

To My Husband Chris

Your love and support
are my motivation and inspiration

-and-

In memory of my son, Jimmy

Table of Contents

ABOUT THE AUTHOR

MARGARET C. JASPER is an attorney engaged in the general practice of law in South Salem, New York, concentrating in the areas of personal injury and entertainment law. Ms. Jasper holds a Juris Doctor degree from Pace University School of Law, White Plains, New York, is a member of the New York and Connecticut bars, and is certified to practice before the United States District Courts for the Southern and Eastern Districts of New York, and the United States Supreme Court.

Ms. Jasper has been appointed to the panel of arbitrators of the American Arbitration Association and the law guardian panel for the Family Court of the State of New York, is a member of the Association of Trial Lawyers of America, and is a New York State licensed real estate broker and member of the Westchester County Board of Realtors, operating as Jasper Real Estate, in South Salem, New York.

Ms. Jasper is the author and general editor of the following legal almanacs: Juvenile Justice and Children's Law; Marriage and Divorce; Estate Planning; The Law of Contracts; The Law of Dispute Resolution; Law for the Small Business Owner; The Law of Personal Injury; Real Estate Law for the Homeowner and Broker; Everyday Legal Forms; Dictionary of Selected Legal Terms; The Law of Medical Malpractice; The Law of Product Liability; The Law of No-Fault Insurance; The Law of Immigration; The Law of Libel and Slander; The Law of Buying and Selling; Elder Law; The Right to Die; AIDS Law; The Law of Obscenity and Pornography; The Law of Child Custody; The Law of Debt Collection; Consumer Rights Law; Bankruptcy Law for the Individual Debtor; Victim's Rights Law; Animal Rights Law; Workers' Compensation Law; Employee Rights in the Workplace; Probate Law; Environmental Law; Labor Law; The Americans with Disabilities Act; The Law of Capital Punishment; Education Law; The Law of Violence Against Women; Landlord-Tenant Law; Insurance Law; Religion and the Law; Commercial Law; Motor Vehicle Law; Social Security Law; The Law of Drunk Driving; The Law of

Speech and the First Amendment; Employment Discrimination Under Title VII; Hospital Liability Law; Home Mortgage Law Primer; Copyright Law; Patent Law; Trademark Law; Special Education Law; The Law of Attachment and Garnishment; Banks and their Customers; and Credit Cards and the Law.

INTRODUCTION

This legal almanac explores the area of law known as elder law. Elder law encompasses the issues which are of common interest to senior citizens, including legal, financial, and health care concerns, and retirement and estate planning. This legal almanac is intended to provide information which will give senior citizens a general understanding of their rights under the law, and includes a general discussion of such pertinent areas as pensions, investing, retirement planning, purchasing life insurance, making a will, insurance and health care choices, and age discrimination.

Senior citizens also deal with the same day-to-day legal issues facing all citizens. Thus, it is important for the senior citizen to be aware of his or her legal rights and responsibilities. However, this almanac is not meant to take the place of professional legal advice. When confronted with a legal problem or question, the senior citizen is advised to seek counsel from an attorney who specializes in the particular area of law at issue.

There are many instances unique to the senior citizen which are complex and may require the advice of a lawyer who is also proficient in those areas unique to elder law practice. For example, senior citizens must deal with private employers and government agencies concerning their benefits, such as retirement pensions, social security, disability, medicare and other entitlements. Professional assistance may be invaluable in cutting through the complexities of the system and making sure they receive everything they are entitled to under the law.

In addition, by the time an individual reaches this stage in life, he or she is likely to have amassed a substantial amount of property, including real and personal property, investments, savings, pensions, and other valuable assets. In this connection, it is wise to seek the advice of a lawyer to assist the senior citizen in making sure their assets are working for them while they are still alive, and in devising an effective plan for the disposition of their property, so that it is distributed according to their wishes upon death.

Seniors citizens may also be confronted with proceedings which seek to place restraints on their civil liberties, such as guardianship, conservatorship, and civil commitment proceedings, as discussed in this almanac. Further, senior citizens must be aware of their rights when faced with age discrimination in such areas as employment, housing, and obtaining credit. In such situations, it is imperative that the senior citizen have adequate legal representation to protect his or her constitutional rights.

The above examples are only some of the legal issues a senior citizen may confront which may require the assistance of a lawyer. Of particular concern to the senior citizen on a fixed income is the cost of seeking professional advice—often a deterring factor in obtaining legal assistance. However, there are many public and private organizations which offer affordable or free legal services to senior citizens. One may obtain information from the state and local bar associations, as well as the Legal Aid Society for their locale.

A directory of national legal services for the elderly is set forth at Appendix 1. Directories of state offices of aging and national organizations which promote the rights of senior citizens are also set forth in Appendix 2 and 3, and may be a valuable resource for further information.

The Appendix also provides sample documents and other pertinent information and data. The Glossary contains definitions of many of the terms used throughout the almanac.

CHAPTER 1:
RETIREMENT PLANNING

IN GENERAL

Many people have three sources of income at retirement: Social Security benefits; employee pension benefits; and personal savings. Unfortunately, a great many retired people lack one or more of those income sources, and a large number of people rely solely on social security benefits to see them through their retirement years.

This can be a problem, since Social Security was intended from its inception to supplement other sources of income, not to comfortably provide a living in itself. To avoid financial hardship, it is important to start planning for your retirement years at an early age.

To plan for retirement, the first thing you need to do is figure out how much money you and, if you are married, your spouse need to live comfortably. This figure may not be easy to determine. Remember to take into account future changes in prices and living expenses.

If you are satisfied with your present standard of living, you can determine a comparable target figure by multiplying your current income, after taxes are deducted, by the number of years you will be in retirement—approximately 20 years for most people. This is a rough estimate of the amount of money you will need to retire comfortably.

Keep in mind, however, that many factors may alter the amount of money you will need in retirement as compared to the amount of money you need to cover your expenses today. For example, putting your children through college is a major expenditure that will not figure into your retirement living expenses. If your home will be fully paid for prior to retirement, your current mortgage is another expense you will not have to worry about at that time. In determining your target amount, you also should not deduct the money you may be putting aside each week in your savings account, because you most likely will not be doing that during your retirement years.

On the other hand, you must consider the effects of inflation. By the time you retire, your dollar will not buy as much as it does today. Since nobody can determine precisely what the rate of inflation will be between now and the day you retire, you will have to calculate a reasonable figure per year, based on past statistics.

Calculate your expected Social Security benefits, and benefits from your pension, if you expect to earn one, in order to estimate how much you will need to save during your working years to supplement your income and achieve your desired standard of living for retirement. Remember that your personal savings and investments will be earning interest during this time, which will help you achieve your goal. The target figure you set may seem difficult to achieve, but if you start planning your financial future today, you should be able to ensure yourself a comfortable retirement.

The various methods of financing your retirement, such as through employee or personal retirement plans, personal investing, and social security, are set forth below.

EMPLOYEE PENSION PLANS

An employee pension plan is a program established and maintained by an employer primarily to provide systematically for the payment of benefits to an employee, or the employee's beneficiaries, over a period of years after the employee's retirement. The amount of the retirement benefits paid by the pension plan is based on such factors as length of employment and salary. The amount of pension benefits you are eligible to receive can be a major factor in planning for your retirement years.

Eligibility

If your employer offers a pension plan, there are certain criteria you must generally meet in order to receive benefits at retirement, such as length of employment, and age at retirement.

It is important to be familiar with all aspects of your employer's pension plan so that you can best plan for your retirement. Unlike Social Security retirement benefits, pension benefits are often taxable income to recipients, a factor you should take into consideration when planning your estate.

Vesting

Some pension plans are vested plans. This means that plan participants are guaranteed payment, even if they choose to leave their employment.

If your pension rights are fully vested, you are usually entitled to receive your full pension, based on your length of service, when you leave your place of employment.

If your plan is partially vested, you are entitled to receive partial pension benefits if you leave your employment before retirement age. If your pension is not vested, however, you will not receive anything when you leave your employment, except repayment of your own contributions to the plan, if any.

In 1974, Congress enacted the Employee Retirement Income Security Act of 1974 (ERISA). ERISA was enacted to protect the interests of employees in connection with their pension plans and other work-related benefits. The statute is complex, but employees should be aware of its basic provisions. Under ERISA, those who are responsible for operating a retirement plan, known as plan administrators, are obligated to provide employees with important facts about the employer's pension plan, in writing and free of charge.

ERISA also requires employers to provide vesting rights within certain specified time limits, although an employer can grant vesting rights earlier. Under ERISA, employers are given three alternatives to comply with the vesting requirement:

1. Ten Year Vesting—Full vesting is achieved after ten years of credited service. This means that your pension will be fully vested after you have worked for your employer for ten years.

2. Graded vesting—This provides for vesting of 25% of benefits after five years of credited service, vesting of an additional 5% per year of benefits after another five years of service, and vesting of an additional 10% for each year thereafter. This means that your plan is 50% vested after ten years of employment, and your plan will be fully vested after fifteen years of employment.

3. Rule 45 Vesting—Vesting according to Rule 45 means that 50% vesting must be given when the total of an employee's age and length of employment equals 45, as long as the length of service is at least five years. In addition, vesting rights increase 10% each year after the 50% level is reached until full vesting is attained. In any event, under Rule 45 vesting, employees must be given their 50% vesting rights after ten years of employment regardless of their age.

PERSONAL RETIREMENT PLANS

If your employer does not provide a pension plan, it would be prudent to set up your own personal retirement account. There are two main types of personal retirement accounts available. Employees who have no pension plan through their employer may set up what is known as an Individual Retirement Account (IRA). Persons who are self-employed may invest in Keogh plans.

IRA and Keogh plans are similar in many ways. They are both retirement plans you fund yourself from your own savings. Both plans afford the investor a tax deferral as an incentive to save money for their retirement. This tax deferral allows you to build up your savings more quickly. Any withdrawal from the account will be taxed, but interest earned on the principal is not taxed until retirement. It is worth noting, however, that you will most likely begin withdrawing money from your account only after your retirement, when you will probably be in a lower tax bracket.

Another advantage of investing money in an IRA or Keogh plan is that, upon your death, the funds in the plan are not subject to probate and go directly to the beneficiary you named on the account when you opened it. However, the amount of funds in the plan will be included in your taxable estate.

Individual Retirement Accounts

The IRA plan has a monetary contribution cap of $2,000 dollars per year provided you have earned income of $2,000 or more. If you earn less than $2,000, you can contribute up to the amount you earned. There are exceptions to the annual limit in certain situations.

For example, a married couple can contribute up to $4,000 per year provided their total income exceeds $4,000 per year.

One additional situation in which contributions to an IRA may be made is where you change jobs before you are ready to retire, and receive a lump sum payment from your former employer's pension plan. In such a case, you may deposit that lump sum into your IRA account regardless of the amount.

Keogh Plans

The Keogh plan, also known as the H.R. 10 plan, was enacted into law in 1962. The Keogh plan was designed for the self-employed person, and is a retirement vehicle often used by professionals, such as attorneys and physicians, as well as small business organizations.

Unlike the IRA, the Keogh plan allows investors to annually contribute up to $30,000 or 25% of earned income, whichever is less. There is also a special kind of Keogh plan, called a defined benefit plan, to which you may make higher annual contributions.

Fees and Penalties

When shopping around for the personal retirement account best suited to your needs, be sure to inquire about any applicable fees and commissions. Keep in mind that penalties will be assessed if you attempt to withdraw money from your retirement plan before you reach the age of 59, unless you suffer a total disability. Of course, any amount you withdraw must be added to your taxable income for that year. Upon your death, your heirs can withdraw money from your account without penalty. You must start withdrawing your money by age 70 to avoid additional penalties.

PERSONAL INVESTING

An investment is defined as an expenditure to acquire property or other assets in order to produce revenue. The collective term for all of your property and financial assets is your portfolio. Usually, the riskier the investment, the higher the rate of return. In retirement, as well as the years approaching retirement, however, it is best to maintain a conservative portfolio by reducing the risk factor associated with your investments.

It is also important to keep a certain portion of your portfolio liquid. A liquid investment is one that is immediately convertible to cash. This may be important in the event you have an emergency need for funds. Without liquid assets, you might be forced to sell a piece of real estate in a bad market, or a stock when its value is down, and as a result, you would have to take a loss. Common sources of liquid assets that you should consider investing in are savings accounts and certificates of deposit.

Three types of non-liquid investments you might wish to include in your portfolio are stocks, bonds, and annuities.

Stocks

A stock certificate evidences the holder's ownership and proportionate share in a particular business. Stocks are likely to be the riskiest of the investment vehicles in your portfolio. Because stock prices fluctuate dramatically, investing in the stock market offers the potential for both large returns and drastic losses. If you are approaching retirement age, and you previously had a large portion of your portfolio in the stock market, you may want to switch all or most of your investments out of stocks and into one of the more conservative investment vehicles.

You can invest your money in a mutual fund—an investment company that raises money by selling its own stock to the public and investing the proceeds in other securities. The value of the mutual fund's stock fluctuates with that of the securities within its portfolio.

Before buying any stock, you should carefully review the company's background, including its earnings and debt, the dividends it pays, and the growth of the company. You should also assess the viability of the general industry in which the company is situated. For example, the stock of a major automobile manufacturer may appear solid, but if there is a general decline in the automotive industry as a whole, that company may suffer as a result.

Bonds

A bond certificate evidences a debt on which the issuing company or governmental entity promises to pay the holder a specified amount of interest for a specified length of time, and to repay the loan on the expiration date. The holder of the bond is a creditor of the corporation unlike a shareholder, who owns stock in the company.

For example, if you buy a $500 bond, you are actually lending $500 to the company or governmental entity that issued the bond. In return, the bond issuer pays you a specified annual rate of interest, such as 10%. On the maturity date of the bond—i.e., the date when the bond matures or becomes payable, your initial investment is returned to you.

If you sell your bond before it matures, you may get back more or less than you initially paid for the bond, depending on the interest rates at that time. Thus, if you bought a $500 bond with a specified annual interest rate of 10%, and you wish to sell that bond at a time when interest rates have declined to 7%, you may be able to sell the bond for an amount exceeding $500 because the buyer may want to take advantage of the higher interest rate.

On the other hand, if you bought the same $500 bond with a specified interest rate of 7%, and you wished to sell the bond at a time when similar bonds are yielding interest rates of 10%, you will probably have to sell the bond for less than your initial investment. That is because the buyer will not be willing to pay full price for a bond that yields a lower interest rate than bonds currently being issued.

The interest you earn on corporate bonds is taxable. Federal bonds are taxable by the federal government, but not by state or local governments. The interest on state and local government bonds is usually exempt both from federal tax and any taxes payable to the state or local government that issued the bond.

Bonds, although less risky than stocks, do involve some risk. The measure of risk is tied into the rate of interest you can expect to receive. For example, bonds issued by a strong company usually carry a relatively low annual interest rate, while bonds with a precarious future pay a much higher rate. Before investing in a company's bonds, it is best to investigate the stability of the company. Companies who operate bond-rating services, such as Moody's and Standard & Poor's, are valuable sources of information in this regard.

Annuities

An annuity is the right to receive fixed, periodic payments, either for life, or for a term of years. Simply stated, an annuity is a contract whereby Party #1 pays money to Party #2 in exchange for Party #2's promise to make a series of future payments.

There are variations on this basic principle. For example, many annuities guarantee that you, or your heirs, will receive at least a certain specified amount in case you should die shortly after purchasing the annuity. Some annuities begin paying benefits immediately, while others are deferred, which means you buy the annuity now but don't collect on it until a later date.

An annuity can be fixed or variable. A fixed annuity means that the amount of money you receive each month is the same. A variable annuity provides that your monthly return will fluctuate depending on how well the issuer invests your money, usually with a guaranteed minimum.

Some annuities contain a tax deferral feature. Like Keogh and IRA personal retirement accounts, the interest on a tax deferred annuity is not taxed year by year, but becomes taxable when you actually begin receiving the money. However, unlike Keogh and IRA accounts, the money you put into an annuity cannot be deducted from your gross income for income tax purposes, unless you buy the annuity as part of your plan.

As with any investment, you should shop around to make sure you purchase the annuity that best suits your needs. Check carefully into the provisions relating to fees, penalties, and other charges. Also investigate the financial stability of the annuity company and choose from the companies with the best overall ratings.

Your Rights As An Investor

Before you make any investment, you have the right to obtain all material information about that investment in order to help you make an informed decision. The information you are entitled to receive includes the track record of the business or the individuals involved in the business and all of the factors that are likely to affect the investment vehicle's performance. If a prospectus is available, you should obtain a copy and read it carefully. The prospectus should contain much of the information about the investment, both positive and negative, that you need to make your informed decision.

Other sources of information about investments are various business publications that should be available in your public library. If the company's stock is publicly traded, you are entitled to review its annual report. Do not merely rely on the limited information that appears in the advertisement for the particular investment you are interested in, because such advertisements are likely to feature only the positive aspects of the investment.

Never allow yourself to be pressured into making an investment before you have had a chance to investigate all of the information you need to make an informed decision. It is highly unprofessional for a legitimate investment professional to use such pressure tactics and should alert you to the need to proceed with extreme caution. You should request disclosure of all of the possible costs and obligations that may accompany the investment, including sales commissions, service charges, penalties, and any other transaction expenses.

You should also ask about restrictions on your access to the funds you invest. Some investments may impose time restrictions on access. You should be informed of those restrictions before you invest, to avoid problems at a later date. In addition, you are entitled to receive information about the status of your investment at any time. Most companies mail monthly statements to investors, but you should also be able to receive accurate information upon request, should you need it.

In any investment, there are risks, some of which are more obvious than others. You should determine all of the potential risks before making your investment. The more obvious risks include declining stock prices and failing businesses. Less obvious risks may include the possibility of losing more money than you initially invested. It is just as important to understand how you can lose money as how you can earn money in an investment. Generally, the higher the potential reward, the greater the potential risk.

SOCIAL SECURITY

Social Security is a national program administered by the Social Security Administration, whereby employees and self-employed persons pay contributions, known as social security taxes, into the program during their working years. The program is administered by the Social Security Administration which has established ten regional offices throughout the country and a number of local offices to serve the needs of the public.

A Directory of Social Security Administration Regional Offices is set forth at Appendix 4.

The amount of social security taxes paid into the program by the employee is a percentage of one's gross salary, up to a designated limit, which is determined by Congress. This tax deduction is often designated as "FICA" on your payroll stub. Your employer is also required to pay social security taxes based on your gross salary.

Social Security taxes are used to pay for all Social Security benefits, including a portion of your Medicare coverage. The money Social Security takes in far exceeds the money it spends. The excess, called the reserve is pooled into special trust funds. The money in those trust funds is invested in Treasury bonds, which the government, by law, is required to pay back with interest.

Although Social Security is most often thought of as a retirement program, many persons are eligible to receive Social Security benefits before retirement age. When a person's earnings stop or are reduced because he or she retires, dies, or becomes disabled, monthly cash benefits are paid to replace part of the earnings the person or his or her dependent family has lost. Although a person may thus be eligible for Social Security benefits at any age, the majority of Social Security recipients—approximately 60%—receive Social Security retirement benefits due to retirement.

When the Social Security retirement benefits program was instituted, it was intended not to provide a comfortable standard of living in retirement, but to supplement income, including personal savings and pension benefits. Unfortunately, many senior citizens are trying to live out their retirement years dependent solely on their Social Security checks. This may be due to the fact that their former employment did not provide a pension, or because they did not save any money during their working years to supplement their social security income.

Social security retirement benefits are generally not subject to income tax. A relatively small number of people in the higher income tax brackets may have to pay some tax on a fraction of their benefits.

During an individual's working years, they are required to contribute to the Social Security system through FICA taxes. When that person retires, the Social Security Administration pays the retiree a monthly benefit. The system is designed to work like a pension plan. The majority of Social Security recipients—approximately 60%—receive Social Security retirement benefits due to retirement.

Eligibility

The Social Security Administration has set age 65 as the retirement age for a person who was born before 1938 to receive full social security retirement benefits (known as "full retirement age"). In the year 2000, the age at which a person's full retirement benefits are payable gradually increased to age 67. For example, those born in 1940 reach "full retirement age" at 65 and 6 months. Individuals born in 1950, reach full retirement age at 66. Anybody born in 1960 or later will not be eligible for full retirement benefits until age 67.

A table depicting the eligibility age for full social security benefits according to year of birth is set forth at Appendix 5.

There are additional eligibility requirements for Social Security. For example, you must have worked for a specified number of years before you are eligible to receive Social Security retirement benefits. The amount of your monthly Social Security benefits is calculated according to a specified formula based on your average earnings over those employment years. Your earnings are tracked according to your Social Security number, which you are required to have if you are working. In fact, the Internal Revenue Service requires that a Social Security number be shown on tax returns for all dependents over the age of one.

As you work and pay Social Security taxes, you earn Social Security "credits," up to a maximum of four credits per year. The amount of money you need to earn one credit goes up each year. Currently, most people need 40 credits to qualify for benefits. Retirement benefits are calculated on earnings during a lifetime of work. During your lifetime, you will probably earn more credits than you need to be eligible for Social Security. However, it is your income, not the number of credits you earn, that determines the amount of your benefit under the Social Security system. Years of high earnings will increase the amount of the benefit. Because benefit computations are based on a person's date of birth and complete work history, there are differences in amounts among recipients.

In most cases, Social Security retirement benefits do not begin the month the person reaches the age of eligibility. Benefits usually begin the following month. To receive retirement benefits, you must have attained the age of eligibility for the entire month. Nevertheless, the law provides that one "attains" their age the day before their birthday. Thus, individuals born on the 1st or 2nd day of the month will usually be eligible for benefits beginning the month of their birth.

Family Benefits

When an individual becomes eligible for retirement benefits, certain family members may also be entitled to receive benefits. However, there is a limit to the amount of money that can be paid to a family. If the total benefits payable to the retiree's spouse and children exceed this limit, their benefits will be reduced proportionately. Nevertheless, the retiree's benefit will not be affected.

As further discussed below, eligible family members may include: (i) a spouse age 62 or older; (ii) a spouse under age 62 if he or she is taking care of the retiree's child who is under age 16 or disabled; (iii) a former spouse; (iv) children up to age 18; (v) children age 18-19 if they are full-time elementary or secondary students; and (vi) children over age 18 if they are disabled.

Spousal Benefits

A spouse is entitled to Social Security even if he or she never worked. If the married couple is over age 65 when the retiree's benefits begin, the spouse may be entitled to receive an additional amount equal to 50 percent of the retiree's benefit. A spouse may begin collecting benefits prior to age 65 provided the retiree is receiving benefits. However, if the spouse begins collecting benefits before age 65, his or her benefit is permanently reduced by a percentage based on the number of months before he or she reaches age 65.

For example, a spouse who begins collecting benefits at age 65 would receive approximately 46 percent of the retiree's full retirement benefit. If that spouse begins collecting at age 63, the benefit amount would be reduced to approximately 42 percent, etc. Nevertheless, if the retiree's spouse is taking care of a child who is under the age of 16 or disabled and receiving Social Security benefits, the spouse is entitled to full benefits regardless of age.

If both spouses worked and are eligible for their own social security benefits, the SSA always pays the individual benefit first. However, if the individual's benefit as a spouse is higher than their retirement benefit, he or she will get a combination of benefits equaling the higher spouse benefit.

For example, if a husband qualifies for his own retirement benefit of $250 and a wife's benefit of $400, at age 65, he will receive his own $250 retirement benefit plus $150 from the wife's benefit for a total of $400. However, if he decides to take his own retirement benefit before reaching full retirement age, both benefit amounts will be reduced.

A divorced spouse is also entitled to receive benefits on a former mate's Social Security record if the marriage lasted at least 10 years. The divorced spouse must be age 62 or older and unmarried. If the spouse has been divorced at least two years, he or she can get benefits even if the worker is not yet retired. However, the worker must have enough credits to qualify for benefits and be age 62 or older. The amount of benefits a divorced spouse receives has no effect on the amount of benefits a current spouse may obtain.

Unmarried Children Benefit

When an individual retires, monthly Social Security payments may also be made to unmarried children under age 18, or age 19 if still in elementary or secondary school, or children age 18 or over who were severely disabled before age 22 and who continue to be disabled. Each eligible child generally receives up to one-half of the retiree's full benefit.

Applying for Retirement Benefits

The SSA advises people to apply for retirement benefits 3 months before they want their benefits to begin. Even if an individual does not intend to retire, he or she should still sign up for Medicare 3 months before reaching age 65.

An application for social security retirement benefits can be made by calling the SSA or by visiting one of the offices. The SSA's toll-free telephone number is 1-800-772-1213. People who are deaf or hard of hearing may call the SSA's toll-free "TTY" number, 1-800-325-0778. The applicant has the right to designate a representative to act on his or her behalf in dealing with the SSA by filing an Appointment of Representative (SSA Form 1696-U4). The representative must also accept the appointment by signing the form.

It is important to select an individual who is qualified to act in this capacity as he or she will have the authority to act on the applicant's behalf in most Social Security matters. Often, the appointee will be an attorney who is familiar with the Social Security system.

The following information and original or certified copies of listed documents will be needed to process the application:

1. The applicant's Social Security number;

2. The applicant's birth certificate;

3. The applicant's W-2 forms or self-employment tax return for the last year;

4. The applicant's military discharge papers if he or she had military service;

5. The applicant's spouse's birth certificate and Social Security number if the spouse is applying for benefits;

6. The applicant's children's birth certificates and Social Security numbers, if applying for children's benefits;

7. Proof of U.S. citizenship or lawful alien status if the applicant—or the applicant's spouse or child if applying for their benefits—was not born in the U.S.; and

8. The name of the applicant's bank and account number so the benefits can be directly deposited into the account.

Retiring Before Full Retirement Age

If you wish, you may retire before full retirement age and receive Social Security retirement benefits at a rate which is reduced a small percentage for each month before you reach that age. However, the earliest age you can start collecting benefits is 62. Benefits are reduced five-ninths of one percent for each month you are retired before age 65, up to a maximum of 20 percent for people who retire the month they reach 62.

For example, if you sign up for Social Security at 62 years of age, you will receive approximately 80% of your full retirement benefit. At 64 years of age, you will receive 93-1/3% of your full retirement benefit.

It is important to note that your benefit is permanently reduced if you elect to start receiving it earlier than your full retirement age. The advantage to early retirement is that you begin to receive benefits before full retirement age and thus receive them for a longer period of time.

Working Beyond Retirement Age

Some senior citizens continue to work full-time beyond full retirement age, and do not sign up for Social Security. Delaying retirement can increase your Social Security benefit by increasing your average earnings and will earn you a special credit from the Social Security program. This credit takes the form of a designated percentage added to the retiree's Social Security benefit depending on year of birth.

These increases are added in automatically from the time the individual reaches full retirement age until he or she starts receiving benefits, or until age 70. For example, an individual born in 1943 or later will receive an additional 8 percent per year to their benefit for each year of delayed retirement beyond full retirement age.

A table depicting the percentage of increase in social security benefits for each year of delayed retirement beyond full retirement age according to year of birth is set forth at Appendix 6.

Individuals who return to work after they start receiving benefits may be able to receive a higher benefit based on those earnings. This is because Social Security automatically recomputes the benefit amount after the additional earnings are credited to the individual's earnings record.

Nevertheless, some individuals who continue to work after retirement age, while also receiving benefits, may have their social security benefits reduced or eliminated depending on their earnings. Currently, this provision only affects people under the age of 70, and the reduction only applies to earned income.

In 1998, the earnings limit was $9,120 for people under age 65, and $14,500 for people age 65 through 69. An individual can still receive their entire social security benefit provided their earnings do not exceed the designated limit. As set forth below, if the earnings exceed the designated limit, some or all of the social security benefit may be withheld. For individuals under age 65, the SSA deducts $1.00 in benefits for each $2.00 earned above $9,120. For individuals age 65 through 69, the SSA will deduct $1.00 in benefits for each $3.00 earned above $14,500.

Individuals are required to report their earnings up to age 70. In the year a recipient reaches age 70, they are only responsible for reporting their earnings for the months before the month they reach age 70. A recipient does not have to report their earnings if they are 70 or older.

Social security retirement benefits are not affected by income you may earn as a result of investments or savings you have set aside to supplement your retirement income.

Every year, the SSA sends recipients an SSA-1099 form showing how much they received in the past year. This form can be used as proof of the benefit amount. SSA also sends a notice when the benefit amount increases because of an annual cost of living raise.

Effect of Employment Pension Benefits on Social Security Benefits

If an individual receives a retirement pension from their employment, and also paid social security taxes, their retirement pension will not affect their Social Security benefit. However, pensions from work that is not covered by Social Security—such as federal civil service employment and some state or local government systems—may reduce the amount of one's Social Security benefit.

Representative Payees

If a family member entitled to receive Social Security or SSI benefits is legally incompetent or otherwise mentally or physically incapable of managing his or her benefits, another individual may be designated by the SSA to receive that family member's social security benefits. The designated individual is known as a "representative payee."

Although a friend or custodial institution—e.g., a nursing home—can be designated as a representative payee, the SSA prefers to appoint relatives who are personally concerned for the beneficiary. The Social Security or SSI benefits are sent directly to the representative payee who must manage the funds for the personal care and well-being of the beneficiary, and pay the beneficiary's bills from the funds.

Any remaining funds do not belong to the representative payee, but must be saved for the benefit of the recipient. The representative payee is obligated to report certain changes in the beneficiary's circumstances that could affect their continuing eligibility to receive benefits.

SUPPLEMENTAL SECURITY INCOME

Senior citizens who haven't worked long enough to be eligible for Social Security, or whose benefits are very low, may be eligible to receive additional benefits under another government program entitled Supplemental Security Income (SSI). General tax revenues from the U.S. Treasury are used to finance the SSI program.

In order to be eligible for SSI payments, your income and assets must fall below certain established limits. Not all assets are taken into account. For example, your home and personal belongings are not counted, but bank accounts and cash on hand are included in the calculation.

Although SSI is a federal program, some states supplement the national payments and have established higher SSI rates and allow higher income limits than others. It is important, therefore, to ascertain your individual state's eligibility for the SSI program. Unlike the income limits, however, the SSI asset limits do not vary among the states.

CHAPTER 2:
ESTATE PLANNING

IN GENERAL

Planning your estate is preparing for your future. It basically involves the coordination of your financial affairs in order to provide future economic security for yourself and your family. It thus encompasses the creation, conservation and disposition of your estate, or net worth. Depending on the size of your estate, effective estate planning may be quite complex, or it may be as uncomplicated as the preparation of a simple will, along with a review of your benefits and insurance provisions. Nevertheless, for the security of your family, planning is equally as important regardless of the size of your estate.

Planning your estate gives you some control over the disposition of your assets and the carrying out of your wishes following your death. Often, senior citizens are the sole caretaker of grandchildren or other minor children. Planning your estate allows you to provide for the guardianship of those minor children. It also permits you to explain to your loved ones why you made certain decisions and distributed your assets in the designated manner. This helps to avoid conflicts among your family and friends after your death, a not uncommon occurrence.

Without adequate planning, your assets will be divided according to the statutes of the state in which you reside, in a manner that may be contrary to your wishes. Some of the major areas you should consider in planning your estate are set forth below.

MAKING A WILL

A will is the legal declaration of a person's wishes for the disposition of his or her possessions after death. The primary purpose for making a will is to ensure that your property is distributed to the people you want to receive it, in the manner and proportion you designate.

A sample will is set forth at Appendix 7.

If you are concerned about how your estate will be distributed after you die, you must execute a will. If you believe you have not accumulated enough assets to justify making a will, you should consider executing a simple will. It is possible that because of the circumstances surrounding your death, your estate will be entitled to a sum of money. In that case, if there were no will, the money would be distributed according to state statute, which might conflict with any plans you would have made had you known you would have assets to pass on to your loved ones.

Further, leaving a will may prevent the dissension, confusion, and bitterness within your family that may occur when your estate is distributed according to statute, rather than according to your clearly expressed and explained directions. To avoid these problems, no matter what your financial situation may be, you should consider making your wishes known by executing a will.

If you die without a will—that is, intestate—your property will probably be distributed to your family members, but it might not be distributed according to your desires. Your will should be tailored to your own particular needs and those of your family. You should consider executing a will, however, even if you have no immediate family.

If you die intestate, your estate will be distributed according to the inheritance laws of the state in which you live. When it is determined that a person has died intestate, his or her estate must be distributed according to the state's statutes concerning intestate succession—the law of descent and distribution. Although state statutes are not uniform in this regard, most provide that the estate passes in varying percentages to the decedent's spouse and children. If the decedent was not married and had no children, the estate usually passes to the decedent's siblings and/or parents.

A table of the state rules of inheritance is set forth at Appendix 8.

Your will, and any other information or documentation that will be needed shortly after your death, such as burial arrangements and the deed to your cemetery plot, should not be kept in a safe deposit box since a bank may deny access to your safe deposit box until it can be opened in the presence of the proper authorities. However, you should keep these items in a safe place and make your family members or other trusted persons aware of their location.

Requirements for Making a Will

There are certain requirements that must be followed in order to make a valid will, which may vary from state to state. Generally, in order to make a valid will, you must be of the required legal age and mentally fit. Each state has a minimum age requirement for making a will. The majority of states, as well as the Uniform Probate Code, designate age 18 as the minimum age for making a will.

There are also technical requirements for the drafting of a valid will, according to your state's law. Generally, the will must be typewritten, signed before two or three witnesses, and dated. The will must also include the appointment of an executor—the person you name to carry out your wishes. Wills do not have to be notarized, but in some states, the witnesses can sign and have notarized a "self-proving affidavit," which eliminates the need for a witness to testify at the probate proceedings.

In certain instances, a will can be successfully contested. The most common reason for a successful will contest is proof of the testator's lack of mental capacity at the time he or she executed the will. In addition, if it can be shown that a will, or any of its parts, was executed under undue influence—i.e., by coercion or force—the will, or that part of it executed under undue influence, is void. Moreover, if a will does not meet all of the legal requirements of the applicable state's statutes, it must be declared void.

Probate

Probate is the process by which a will is determined by a court to fulfill the legal requirements set forth by the state. Probating a will is a largely administrative procedure. The first step is to file the will with the proper court—called the "probate," "surrogate," or "chancery" court, depending on the state. The deceased's property is then accumulated and inventoried, and any debts, including taxes, are paid. Creditors are given a certain amount of time to make their claims, after which all claims are barred. The remainder of the property left in the estate after payment of claims is distributed according to the will (or according to the state intestacy laws, if there is no valid will). Some debts, such as liens on certain assets, like real estate or automobiles, are not paid from the estate, but are assumed by the inheritor of the particular asset.

Because the probate process can be time-consuming and expensive, there is growing support for probate reform. In the United States, there are legal mechanisms for property to bypass a will, also known as probate avoidance methods. Until reform is achieved in this country, many persons will continue to attempt to avoid it or to minimize the portions of their estates that are subject to the probate process.

Life insurance proceeds are an example of assets that do not pass by will. In addition, any property held in joint tenancy by the deceased passes directly to the other joint tenants, each of whom is deemed to have an equal interest in the property. Married couples commonly hold deeds to marital real estate and bank accounts as joint tenants.

A form of real estate ownership, available only to married couples, is tenancy by the entirety. This type of arrangement also avoids probate, since each of the spouses is considered to hold title to the whole property and the death of one spouse does not affect the other spouse's ownership of the whole property. Similar to a joint tenancy, a tenancy by the entirety is grounded in the common-law theory that a husband and wife are one person.

Some states provide various exemptions from the probate process by either allowing a certain amount of the deceased's property to be completely exempt from probate or subject to a much more simplified probate process than normal.

Families often resort to what is known as informal probate avoidance, whereby the family bypasses the court and independently divides the deceased relative's property as his or her will—if there is one—directs. If there is no will, the family may divide the property according to the state's intestacy statutes or by mutual agreement.

This often happens where the deceased's estate is very small, generally consisting entirely of personal property that is accessible to the family members. However, if the deceased has left any property that requires legal authority to transfer title, such as a house, formal probate procedures must be followed to obtain the legal authority to transfer title.

A table of state law exceptions to conventional probate is set forth at Appendix 9.

The Uniform Probate Code (UPC) was drafted by the National Conference of Commissioners on Uniform State Laws and approved in 1969 by the American Bar Association in response to a public outcry for probate reform. The UPC's purpose is to simplify and make uniform the law of wills and estates among the states, and to promote the speedy, efficient and cost-effective administration of estates. The majority of the states have not yet enacted the UPC, although many states have adopted portions of the law or have enacted their own legislation patterned after UPC provisions.

The Executor

One of the most important aspects of a will is naming your executor, the person who will administer your estate. Your executor should be someone you trust, and who you are reasonably certain will agree to serve in this capacity. Depending on the size of your estate, the tasks the executor may have to perform can be numerous. For example, the executor is responsible for locating all of your assets and disposing of those assets according to your wishes. If your estate has any claim it can assert against a third party—such a claim for the pain and suffering endured prior to death if you were to die in an automobile accident—your executor is responsible for seeing that the claim is pursued. Your executor is responsible for hiring an attorney to represent your claim and collecting any monies which would be due your estate as a result of a settlement or judgment. Your executor is also responsible for seeing that any claims that are made against your estate are satisfied in a manner most advantageous to your estate.

It is important to name back-up executors, in case your first choice is unable or unwilling to serve as executor. Over the years, you should update your will according to the availability of the executor you have named. If a named executor dies, or is otherwise unable to serve, you should amend your will to provide for a new executor. The aim is to avoid a situation where your named executor is unable to serve and the court has to appoint someone to administer your estate. A court-appointed administrator is generally paid out of the proceeds of the estate, which could impact on his or her ability to effectively administer your estate.

It would be prudent to leave your executor sufficiently detailed instructions and information to permit him or her to carry out your wishes in the manner most beneficial for your estate. You can provide this information in the form of a letter attached to your will. It is important to frequently review and update the information in this letter including all pertinent financial data, as needed.

Careful recordkeeping can also assist the executor in administering your will. For example, if you keep complete and detailed tax records, your executor will be better able to handle any claims made against your estate by the taxing authorities that might otherwise be inexplicable. You should also keep accurate records and books concerning any loans you may have made or debts you may have incurred, so that your executor can collect on monies payable to your estate and avoid paying out fraudulent claims against your estate.

Make sure you keep ownership documents and records—such as titles, deeds, and other receipts—along with an up-to-date inventory of all of your property and assets, in a safe place. It is a good idea to disclose this location in the instruction letter to your executor.

Your Beneficiaries

The beneficiaries you name in your will are those persons, or entities, you wish to receive gifts of your property upon your death. A primary beneficiary is your first choice to receive a specified gift of property. Alternate beneficiaries can be named to receive that specific property if the primary beneficiary predeceases you and you do not amend your will to change the primary beneficiary. Residuary beneficiaries are the persons or entities which receive the balance of your estate, if any, after all of the specific gifts of property are made. If alternate beneficiaries are not named for any specific gift of property, and the primary beneficiary predeceases you, that property will pass to the residuary beneficiary.

It is important to provide for a survivorship period—a specified period of time during which the beneficiary must survive you in order to inherit under your will. If your primary beneficiary dies shortly after you, and there is no established survivorship period, the property intended for your primary beneficiary will pass under his or her will and possibly end up in the hands of strangers. If you provide for a survivorship period and your primary beneficiary dies within that time period, however, the property will pass instead to the alternate or residuary beneficiary under your will.

If you plan to leave property to a minor child, you must be aware that any substantial gift must be supervised by an adult guardian who must be named in your will. This adult guardian is obligated to use the money you leave to provide for the needs of the child, and generally must regularly report to the court on how the money is being spent, and must receive permission of the court before investing the property. When the child reaches the age of majority, the guardianship relationship automatically ends and the child is entitled to receive the remainder of his or her property. Property can also be left to minor children by means of a trust, as discussed below.

Disinheritance

With few exceptions, you are not required to leave any property to any person unless you wish to do so. Simply do not name those persons in your will, and they will have no claim to your property after you die. You are thus permitted to disinherit any of your children, although you must make that intention clear in your will or that child may make a claim against your estate. To disinherit a child, you can either expressly state your intention to do so by including such a clause in your will or you can leave that child a very small gift, such as one dollar, which, for all practical purposes, would constitute a disinheritance.

Disinheriting your spouse is more complicated. Carefully check your state's laws before attempting such a disinheritance. In the majority of states, you simply cannot disinherit your spouse unless your spouse waives his or her right to a portion of your estate. In the absence of such a waiver, your spouse is generally entitled to at least one-third of your estate. In community property states, however, a spouse is not legally entitled to insist on any share of a deceased spouse's estate.

Need for Periodic Review of Your Will

There may be changes in your situation during your lifetime that require you to revise and update your will. You should thus make a point of reviewing your will on a regular basis, particularly if there have been any major changes in your life, such as an addition to your family, an increase in income or assets, or a need to change your beneficiaries. In addition, if you move out of state, you should check to make sure your will conforms to the requirements of the new state.

You can revise your will simply by making a new will. If the changes are minor, you may prefer to prepare a separate document—known as a codicil—to make the additions or deletions. The codicil must be executed in the same manner as the will in order to be valid. To avoid any risk of confusion, however, it is advisable to prepare a new will, which should expressly state that it revokes any prior wills and codicils.

A sample codicil to a will is set forth at Appendix 10.

Estate Administration

If the decedent died without a valid will, he or she did not provide for an executor. In such a case, the court will appoint a person to administer the decedent's estate, often a member of the immediate family. The administrator carries out all of the duties that would have been incumbent on the executor if there had been a will, such as: (1) making an inventory and valuation of all of the assets of the decedent; (2) paying out any debts and taxes owed; (3) instituting lawsuits for any claims the estate may have against third parties and collecting any resulting judgments or settlements in such actions; and (4) defending the estate against any lawsuits and claims. Once the estate is administered, the balance is distributed to the decedent's beneficiaries according to the applicable state statutes.

ESTABLISHING TRUSTS

A trust is the voluntary transfer of real or personal property, known as the trust corpus, trust assets, or trust principal, by a person—the creator or settlor of the trust—to a another party, known as the trustee.

The trustee is obligated to manage and invest the trust principal and to pay the trust income—and sometimes the trust principal, where trust income is insufficient—to or for the benefit of the beneficiaries of the trust, usually free of court intervention. For these reasons, you should name as your trustee a person you believe will be able to adequately and reliably manage the trust.

A trust may be used to provide financial security for your family, to avoid the time-consuming and expensive probate process after your death, and in some cases, to minimize taxes. A trust can be particularly useful in providing for minor children, handicapped relatives, and any of your loved ones who may have special needs.

There are many kinds of trusts. One which is created by will to take effect at the time of your death is called a testamentary trust. If the trust is created during your lifetime, it is called an inter vivos, or living trust, and may be irrevocable or revocable, depending on the creator's retention of control over the trust.

ESTATE TAXATION

Federal Estate Tax

Federal estate tax, also known as death tax, is the tax imposed on the right to transfer property by death. Thus, the responsible party for paying estate tax is the decedent's estate, not the inheritors of the property. All property owned by the deceased may be subject to payment of federal estate taxes, whether or not the transfer avoids probate, including life insurance.

Presently, if the value of your gross estate is over $675,000, an estate tax return must be filed. However, since the filing requirement is based on your gross estate, and does not take into account items such as the allowable exemptions, taxes will not necessarily be due. To determine whether your estate will incur federal estate tax, you should first estimate the net worth of your property. You should then deduct the allowable exemptions, including: (1) the marital deduction, which provides an exemption for all property left to your surviving spouse; (2) the charitable organization exemption, which provides an exemption for all gifts made to a tax-exempt charity; and (3) the $675,000 threshold exemption. Keep in mind, however, that any taxable gifts you made during your lifetime can reduce the exemption accordingly. The federal estate tax exemption threshold to scheduled to increase in 2002. The threshold will rise to $1 million by 2006.

State Estate Tax

States are also empowered to impose death taxes on their residents. Generally, such taxes are assessed on the resident's personal property and any real property located in the state. You should check your local statutes to find out if your state imposes death taxes and in which situations such taxes are assessed. Some states assess death taxes only on estates that are subject to federal estate tax, as discussed above. Other states impose an inheritance tax, which is a tax on the inheritor's right to receive property from the estate.

If you maintain residences in more than one state, you may want to establish your domicile in the state that imposes little or no death taxes. Your domicile is the state with which you have the most significant ties, such as the state in which you vote, carry on your business, and own your primary residence.

GUARDIANSHIP AND CONSERVATORSHIP

All persons who have reached the legal age of majority are presumed by law to be legally competent. However, when a person, due to physical or mental incapacity or incompetence, is no longer able to manage his or her affairs, or function safely in society, the individual's family may petition the court to intervene and protect that person and others. Depending on the nature of the incapacity, there are certain proceedings which may be initiated in this regard, as set forth below.

If an individual is unable to manage his or her personal and/or financial affairs, the state may appoint a guardian or conservator who will manage that person's affairs on his or her behalf. The legally incapacitated person is known as a ward of the guardian.

In many jurisdictions, the terms guardian and conservator are used interchangeably. Some jurisdictions appoint the guardian to manage only the ward's personal affairs, and the conservator is appointed to manage the ward's financial affairs. For the purposes of this section, the term guardian is used for simplicity.

The power of the state to take over the affairs of an individual is known as parens patriae under which the state takes the role of parent over the legally incapacitated person, for his or her own protection.

However, any infringement upon one's rights to manage their own affairs must be pursuant to a judicial determination. Thus, before a person can be declared incompetent or incapacitated, a court proceeding must be held in order to determine that the person is suffering from a physical or mental condition which renders that person unable to manage his or her personal and/or financial affairs.

Of course, advanced age is not in and of itself a conclusive factor. People of all ages may be subjected to an incompetency proceeding if their physical or mental capabilities are in question. Nevertheless, guardianship and conservatorship are important issues for many elderly Americans who may at some point suffer from advanced senility, dementia, or the ravages of Alzheimer's disease.

The guardianship proceeding is initiated by the filing of a petition which alleges that the individual is incapable of managing his or her personal and/or financial affairs, and is in need of a guardian or conservator. Notice is required to be given to the senior citizen as well as any other persons required by law to receive notice.

The court will appoint an attorney for the senior citizen who cannot afford legal representation. The court will also appoint a physician to evaluate the physical and mental condition of the senior citizen. An investigation of the senior citizen's personal and financial affairs is also carried out, and the senior citizen, his or her family, friends and other important persons are interviewed.

An informal hearing is subsequently held at which time the court hears all of the testimony and other evidence. The burden of proof lies with the person filing the petition to show that the senior citizen requires a guardian to manage his or her affairs. The standard of proof generally requires clear and convincing evidence.

If, after considering all of the evidence, the court determines that the person is legally incapacitated, a guardian is appointed to manage the ward's affairs. This decision may be appealed, and some states may suspend the appointment of a guardian until the appeal process is exhausted. In addition, the ward may petition for restoration of his or her rights upon a subsequent showing of competency.

Once appointed, the guardian derives certain powers and duties from the applicable state statutes. In some instances, the guardian exercises complete decision making over both the personal and financial affairs of the ward—known as plenary power. This generally includes the right to exercise complete authority over the care, custody and control of the ward.

This power places quite a restraint on the ward, as it may take away previously enjoyed rights, such as the right to vote. Further, it gives the guardian the power to make personal decisions on behalf of the ward, including those concerning living arrangements, medical care, clothing and other needs.

Nevertheless, the evidence may indicate that the ward is incapable of handling his or her financial affairs, but quite capable of making day to day decisions on personal matters. In this case, the guardian's role may be limited to managing the ward's financial affairs, and the ward may retain the right to manage his or her own personal affairs.

Because the appointment of a guardian is a restriction on one's civil liberties, it is a very important determination which should not be ordered unnecessarily.

The appointment of a guardian is not always brought on by a totally involuntary proceeding. The guardian may be someone who the ward appointed prior to his or her incapacitation—e.g., by power of attorney in case the need should arise.

One may appoint an institution, such as a bank, or an individual, such as a family member, to act as guardian. The important criteria is whether the guardian is able to carry out the duties, and has no conflict of interest concerning the ward's affairs.

If the guardian or conservator is involved in the financial affairs of the ward, he or she acts in a fiduciary capacity. Therefore, the law provides for strict reporting requirements. For example, the guardian is generally required to file periodic accountings on the ward's income, property, and the disbursements from the estate. The guardian may also be required to post a bond to protect the estate in case of negligent mismanagement or waste of the estate proceeds.

Civil Commitment

Civil commitment generally refers to the surrender of an individual to the custody of an institution due to serious mental disease or illness. Commitment involves an extraordinary constraint on one's personal liberty, thus, it is often seen as a last resort when the appointment of a guardian or out-patient treatment are not viable alternatives.

The standard required for civil commitment generally requires that the individual be deemed mentally ill or disabled such that a danger exists to the individual, or to others, which is due to the mental illness or disability.

The commitment proceeding is similar to the guardianship proceeding discussed above. A petition is filed by the state or another interested party, notice is given to the individual and other interested parties, and a hearing is scheduled. An attorney will be appointed for anyone who cannot afford legal representation.

An investigation by a psychiatrist or psychologist to assess the individual's mental state will be undertaken. If no alternatives to commitment can be found, a formal hearing is held, usually before a judge. The petitioner presents his or her case, which must satisfy the burden of proof with clear and convincing evidence. If it is determined that the individual should be confined, that decision may be appealed. During confinement, the individual's condition is reviewed periodically to determine whether continued confinement is necessary.

MEDICAL SCIENCE DONATIONS

The rapid advancement of medical science since 1950, particularly in the area of organ transplantation, has given rise to an urgent need for organ donations. Numerous state statutes have been enacted during the past four decades to deal with the accompanying legal issues. Today, the concept of organ donation has become quite common, and all of the states have adopted the Uniform Anatomical Gift Act (UAG). The UAG was promulgated by the National Conference of the Commissioners on Uniform State Laws, with the assistance of the medical profession, to provide guidelines for anatomical donations after death for the use of medical science. By 1972, the Act had been adopted by all 50 states.

Under the UAG, any mentally competent adult can make a donation of his or her body or organs, which becomes effective upon death. In addition, certain authorized persons, usually family members, can authorize such donations according to the Act and pursuant to any additional provisions of the specific state statute.

You can specify the manner in which your anatomical donation is to be carried out and choose from a variety of alternatives. For example, you can donate all or certain parts of your body, and you may set forth your wishes concerning funeral and burial services. The donation must, however, be used for purposes of transplantation, medical or dental research and education, or the advancement of medical or dental science.

There are a number of ways to authorize a medical science donation. The organ donor card permits an individual to indicate the desire to donate organs. In many states, this information is set forth on drivers licenses. The law also recognizes the authority of the deceased's relatives or other persons to authorize donations of the deceased's body or organs. You may also wish to indicate your desire to make an organ or body donation in your will.

LIFE INSURANCE

In General

A life insurance policy is basically a contract between an individual and an insurance company that provides for the payment of a specified sum of money to the beneficiary named in the policy upon the death of the insured. The insurable interest is the life of the insured. The policy is generally purchased in order to minimize the financial impact of the insured's death on his or her beneficiaries, who are usually the insured's spouse and children.

Purchasing life insurance is essential when planning for the financial future of one's family. It is important to seek professional advice from a qualified insurance representative in order to determine how much life insurance one should purchase in order to meet the needs of surviving loved ones upon the insured's death. Of course, one must also consider the cost of purchasing the right amount of insurance coverage that fits within one's budget. It is also important to be aware of mortality rates when evaluating insurance needs.

One basic way to determine how much life insurance to purchase is to first figure out how much income the insured's family would need if he or she died. A rough estimate can be determined by calculating a monthly budget, which should include the following:

Home mortgage, taxes, and insurance;

Household repairs and upkeep;

Utilities;

Food and clothing;

Medical and dental expenses;

Automobile payment, repairs, insurance, and upkeep; and

Miscellaneous expenses.

One should also take into consideration any other income the family will have that may supplement the life insurance income, such as additional earnings, social security income, pension income, or other benefits.

When shopping for insurance, it is important to research the track record of the insurance company you purchase your policy from, and make sure the company is in stable financial condition.

It is important to review one's life insurance policies on a regular basis, particularly if there has been a change in the insured's status, such as a divorce or marriage. One should make sure that the person or persons named as beneficiaries in the policy are those whom the insured wants the insurance proceeds to go to at the time of his or her death. Therefore, one should review and update the named beneficiaries on a regular basis to make sure they are properly designated. One should also periodically review the size of one's estate, including the insurance policy proceeds, to most effectively plan for and reduce the estimated estate taxes, if any.

Types of Life Insurance Policies

There are two basic types of life insurance policies: (i) the term policy; and (ii) the cash value policy.

Term Life Insurance Policy

A term life insurance policy covers the insured for a specified term of one or more years in return for an annual premium. The annual premium may escalate in accordance with one's life expectancy. Death benefits are only paid if the insured dies within the specified term. Some term policies are renewable. However, each time the policy is renewed, the premium increases.

There is no cash value to a term insurance policy during the life of the insured. The policy merely provides a cash benefit to the designated beneficiary upon the insured's death. Some term insurance policies are "convertible," which means that the term policy can be traded for a whole life policy during the conversion period. However, higher premiums will be charged for the new policy.

Cash Value Life Insurance Policy

Unlike the term policy, the cash value life insurance policy usually charges an annual premium that remains the same each year. Cash value policies, while generally more expensive than term policies, offer an additional financial incentive because a portion of the premium is invested and has cash value during the life of the insured. The cash value of the policy may be used to offset premium payments.

In addition, the policyholder may be able to borrow money against the cash value of the policy, which acts as collateral for the loan. The life insurance company generally designates a rate of interest in the policy. However, if the insured dies while a loan is outstanding against the policy, that amount will be deducted from the death benefits. Also, if the insured stops paying the premiums, any outstanding loan amount would be deducted from the cash value payable.

There are also tax benefits to cash value policies in that earnings generated by the policy are generally not taxed while the policy remains in force. If the policyholder decides to stop paying the premiums, he or she can take the specified cash value, also known as the "nonforfeiture benefits" of the policy.

Whole Life Insurance Policy

The most common type of cash value policy is the whole life insurance policy. A whole life policy gives the insured death benefit protection during his or her entire life. The most common whole life policy is known as "straight life" insurance. The same premium is paid for this insurance for as long as the insured lives. Although the premiums for a straight life policy are usually much higher than initial term insurance premiums, in the long run, this type of policy may prove less costly than the term insurance policy, which would become increasingly expensive with each successive renewal.

Another type of whole life policy is one under which the premiums are paid for a specified number of years in return for life-long protection. The premiums for this type of policy, however, are much higher.

Alternative Life Insurance Products

Life insurance policies offering different types of coverage have emerged to give consumers a broader range of choices. As further discussed below, two insurance products growing in popularity are: (i) universal life insurance; and (ii) variable life insurance. Although these policies do not provide the guarantees contained in the more traditional policies, the rate of return may be higher because it is contingent upon the performance of invested premiums.

Universal Life Insurance

Universal life insurance coverage gives policyholders many of the same benefits as whole life policies offer—e.g., cash value and control over premium payments and the amount of death benefit payable—however, they are generally less expensive than whole life coverage. The downside is that the cash value is not guaranteed as it is with the whole life policy, but depends on the performance of invested premium funds.

Variable Life Insurance

Variable life insurance coverage contains many of the same features as universal life coverage, however, the premiums and death benefits are more directly linked to the performance of investments, and policyholders have more control over the manner in which their funds are invested. Therefore, sellers of variable life insurance products are subject to registration with the United States Securities & Exchange Commission.

Probate Avoidance

Insurance proceeds are not subject to the provisions of the deceased's will, nor to the rules of inheritance, thereby avoiding the probate process. Therefore, the proceeds are not part of the deceased's estate, and go directly to the named beneficiary upon the insured's death, with little cost or delay.

However, if the insured names the estate as beneficiary, the proceeds will be paid to the estate. When the named beneficiary is the estate, a lump sum cash payment is usually made by the insurance company and can be used to cover the immediate expenses of the estate without having to resort to the quick and often unprofitable sale of non-liquid assets, such as real estate. It is important to avoid the need for such tactics because when the real estate market is down, the property may have to be sold at a loss.

When the named beneficiary is an individual, there are usually several payout options available at the election of the insured and, sometimes, the beneficiary. For example, the insured may elect to have the proceeds paid out in installments over a specified period of time, with interest. In that case, the interest on the principal is taxable income to the recipient. In the alternative, the insured may elect to have the proceeds applied to the purchase of an annuity to be paid out over the lifetime of the beneficiary. This is particularly useful in the case of a handicapped child who will need lifelong care. Annuities are further discussed below.

Again, it is important to determine what the needs of the surviving family will be upon one's death in order to determine the best payout option. It may be that the family will need more money in the years immediately following the insured's death, in order to make the necessary adjustment to the sudden loss of income, particularly if the insured is the breadwinner of the family, and if there are minor children still in need of support and further education.

Tax Considerations

Although the proceeds from a life insurance policy are normally not subject to income tax, they may be subject to estate tax, depending on the size of the deceased's estate. Currently, an estate must be worth $675,000 or more to be subject to federal estate taxation. Thus, in order for the estate to incur federal estate taxes, the net value of the estate plus the amount of the life insurance proceeds must total at least $675,000. As previously discussed, this amount will begin to rise in 2002.

Transferring Ownership Of The Policy

One way to avoid or reduce federal estate taxes if one's estate is large enough to incur such taxes is to transfer ownership of the life insurance policy. If someone other than the insured owns the policy at the time of the insured's death, the proceeds are not included in the deceased's federal taxable estate.

The owner of a life insurance policy has the right to transfer ownership of the policy to any third party, including the beneficiary. Once ownership of the policy is transferred, however, the insured loses all control over the policy—i.e., the insured can no longer change the named beneficiary of the policy or cancel the policy. Thus, if one spouse transfers ownership of a policy to the other spouse, that spouse continues to own the policy even if there is a subsequent divorce.

There are certain Internal Revenue Service (IRS) rules that can undermine transfer of ownership in some cases. For example, if the insured dies within three years of the transfer, the IRS will disallow the transfer for the purposes of federal estate taxation. Therefore, if one intends to transfer ownership of a life insurance policy, it should be done as early as possible. In addition, if the insured retains any ownership rights or control over the policy— i.e., the "incidents of ownership"—the IRS will include the proceeds of the policy in the deceased's taxable estate. This could result, for example, if one transfers the policy to another, but retains the legal right to perform various acts, such as changing the beneficiaries, canceling the policy, or paying the premiums.

The transfer of a life insurance policy will be considered a gift by the IRS or other taxing authorities, except in the unusual case where the transferee actually pays for the policy. Consequently, transfer of a policy would result in the assessment of a gift tax in an amount determined based on the current value of the policy. Fortunately, however, this tax would be less than the tax assessed if the policy is left in the estate, since the value of the policy during the life of an insured is much less than the proceeds payable under the policy upon the insured's death.

Transferring Ownership to a Trust

Another way to avoid or reduce estate taxes is for the insured to transfer ownership of his or her life insurance policy to a trust, known as an "irrevocable life insurance trust." When an irrevocable life insurance trust is established as a legal entity, the trust becomes the new owner of the policy. Certain requirements govern life insurance trusts. For example, the trust must be irrevocable. If the insured retain any rights to revoke the trust, he or she can be considered the owner of the policy and the proceeds will be included in the taxable estate upon his or her death. In addition, as with the transfer of ownership of a life insurance policy, one cannot be the trustee of the trust. In addition, the trust must be established at least three years prior to the insured's death.

The advantage of naming a trust as the new owner of a life insurance policy is that it avoids some of the risks involved when an individual is named as the owner. For example, since the trust can be instructed to keep the life insurance policy in effect until the insured dies, he or she need not worry that the new owner will fail to pay the premiums, or decide to cash in the policy while the insured is still alive.

Minor Beneficiaries

If you are considering naming minor children, such as your grandchildren, as beneficiaries of a life insurance policy, the proceeds must be overseen by an adult guardian until the minor reaches the legal age of majority. It is imperative that the insured provide for the selection of a guardian to avoid the need for court appointment. There are several ways to designate a guardian.

For example, a guardian of the proceeds can be named in the insured's will. Alternatively, instead of naming a minor as a beneficiary, an adult beneficiary can be named, who will manage the minor's funds until he or she reaches adulthood. However, it is critical that one make sure the adult beneficiary will follow the insured's wishes, and use the money for the benefit of the child. Thus, the adult beneficiary is generally the insured's spouse, a trusted relative, or close friend.

One can also provide for minor children by designating a "living trust" as the beneficiary of the policy, and the children as beneficiaries of that trust. A living trust has the advantages of allowing the insured to provide for the manner in which the proceeds will be used for the children, and also allows the insured to continue the trust until an age deemed appropriate for the child to manage his or her own affairs.

ANNUITIES

The term "annuity" basically refers to a contract between an individual and a financial institution—usually a life insurance company—whereby the insurer, in return for an advance payment of a sum of money, agrees to make periodic payments to the individual for a specified period of time. The specific terms of the annuity are governed by the contract between the individual and the life insurance company. Generally, there is no limit on the amount of funds which can be paid into an annuity contract.

Although annuities have been classified as a type of life insurance, they generally serve a number of other purposes. As discussed above, life insurance is generally purchased to provide security in case of premature death. Annuities, unlike life insurance, basically provide the purchaser security in case of an extended lifespan, and are typically purchased in order to accumulate and protect one's wealth.

Many individuals purchase annuities in order to provide for their retirement, and to make sure that they are financially prepared in case of catastrophe or long-term illness. Others wish to use annuities in order to accumulate wealth to pass on to their heirs while taking advantage of certain tax benefits that annuities provide.

Like life insurance proceeds, an annuity contract passes to the beneficiaries outside of the will, and thus is not subject to probate. The beneficiary of the annuity has the option of keeping the contract in force, thus continuing to defer taxes on the earnings. The policyholder is usually guaranteed a death benefit equal to the greater of the face amount or the market value of the annuity contract.

Fixed Annuities

A "fixed" annuity generally refers to an annuity policy under which the policyholder makes a lump sum payment or series of payments, into an annuity product. Under this traditional type of annuity contract, the named beneficiary is generally entitled to receive a series of annuity payments, which are "fixed" in advance in terms of the amount of payment, the frequency of the distribution, and the duration that such payments will be made.

Dissatisfaction with the low interest rates accompanying fixed annuity products led to a number of alternative investment instruments which yield a more variable return, such as variable annuities and other insurance products. Nevertheless, unlike a fixed annuity, the performance risk of these investments rests with the policyholder and not the insurance company.

Variable Annuities

Variable annuities are more flexible, permitting the owner to take advantage of the favorable taxation of annuities, while also allowing for investment of the annuity payments in a broad range of products. Although this is similar to investment in mutual funds, the variable annuities offer death benefit provisions, and provide insurance that the owner will always be entitled to the face amount of the annuity contract, regardless of the performance of its investments. In addition, although annual fees may be higher for variable annuities, they do not require the up-front fees generally required of mutual funds. Nevertheless, there may be significant withdrawal penalties.

Annuitization

Under the annuity contract, the policyholder may elect to receive guaranteed periodic payments over the policyholder's life, which upon death also continue to be paid to the beneficiary during their lifetime. This is known as "annuitization." A married couple may elect this type of coverage to ensure that the surviving spouse is taken care of following the death of the other spouse. One drawback to annuitization is that once the policyholder and the beneficiary die, the contract ceases to exist and the remaining assets, if any, revert to the insurance company.

An alternative type of annuity contract offering similar protection is a "period certain annuitization" policy under which the policyholder can elect to receive payments for the greater of a guaranteed minimum number of years, or the policyholder's lifetime. For example, if the guaranteed minimum were 15 years, and the policyholder died after 5 years, the beneficiary would receive payments for the remaining 10 years. Alternatively, if the policyholder lived for 25 more years, he or she would receive payments during all 25 years.

In addition, many annuity contracts include "step-up" provisions, which increase the amount of the guaranteed benefit at set intervals, e.g. 5 or 10 years.

Taxation and Penalties

One major benefit of the annuity contract is its minimization of taxation. The annuity contract earnings are exempt from all taxes while the contract is in effect. The owner of the annuity decides when funds will be paid out on the contract. Although disbursements from the account are then subject to taxation, the earnings do not affect social security income.

Annuitization, as discussed above, receives more favorable tax treatment than withdrawing funds from an annuity contract. Annuity payments are generally only taxed at one-half the rate of fund withdrawals. The Internal Revenue Service considers annuity payments to be made up of both earnings and return of the original investment, whereas withdrawals are considered to be earnings which are taxable at ordinary income tax rates.

As with many types of retirement accounts, early withdrawal of annuity funds are subject to penalty. However, funds can remain in the account indefinitely without penalty.

CHAPTER 3:
HEALTH INSURANCE AND LONG-TERM CARE

Private health insurance is a type of insurance employees usually obtain as a benefit of their employment. The employer is generally responsible for paying all or most of the premium payments. Although the employee is generally entitled to choose the type of plan, the employer is entitled to choose the coverage options.

Individuals who work for employers who do not offer health insurance benefits, or who are self-employed, can purchase coverage on their own at generally higher rates. Sometimes unions and professional associations offer their members group rates for health insurance.

Private health insurance plans generally fall under the categories of either (i) traditional health insurance; or (ii) managed care.

Traditional Health Insurance

Traditional health insurance plans—commonly referred to as "fee-for-service" plans—are basically indemnification policies. Under a fee-for-service plan, the insured generally pays a yearly deductible up-front, after which the insurance carrier picks up all or most of the remaining medical expenses for the year.

Under the fee-for-service plan, the insured retains control over choosing their own medical providers, including specialists, without the need for obtaining referrals from a primary physician. The insurance carrier is generally not involved in determining the necessity of the medical treatment.

The disadvantages to fee-for-service plans is that they require the insured to pay more out-of-pocket costs, such as the deductible. In addition, most insurance carriers only pay up to 80% of the remaining medical expenses, leaving the insured responsible for the difference. However, most insurance carriers pay 100% of out-of-pocket expenses once the insured's medical bills reach a specified amount, which is generally quite high.

If the medical provider is one who requires immediate payment, the insured may have to pay the entire bill at the time service is rendered, and then submit it to the carrier for payment of the covered amount.

In addition, insurance carriers generally refer to a chart of "reasonable and customary" medical costs, which is based on the average amount charged for similar services by other medical providers in the area. If the medical provider is one who does not adhere to such a chart, he or she may also seek the difference from the insured.

Managed Care

The majority of private health insurance coverage available today contains some type of managed care plan. Managed care plans generally involve an agreement between an insurance carrier and a selected network of health care providers. There are significant financial incentives offered to the insured if they use the selected providers according to the type of plan and the procedure set forth under the specific plan.

The four basic types of managed health care plans include the: (i) Health Maintenance Organization (HMO); (ii) Preferred Provider Organizations (PPO); (iii) Exclusive Provider Organization (EPO); and (iv) Point-of-Service Plans (POS).

Health Maintenance Organization (HMO)

A Health Maintenance Organization is generally the least flexible type of managed care health plan. Under this plan, the insured is required to visit only those medical providers within the HMO plan. The HMO may be located in a central medical facility where all of the plan medical providers operate, or may consist of a network of individual offices.

Under an HMO plan, the insured must obtain permission from their assigned primary care physician before seeking medical care from a specialist. Further, if the insured seeks medical treatment from medical providers outside of the plan, he or she must generally bear the expense without reimbursement.

The advantage of an HMO plan is that the co-payment, if any, is very small, and the premiums are very low. In addition, the HMO generally offers the insured complete preventive medical care.

Preferred Provider Organization (PPO)

Under a Preferred Provider Organization plan, the insured is given a financial incentive to seek medical care from one of the medical providers in the insurer's selected network. For example, an insured typically pays a small co-payment for medical treatment by a network medical provider, e.g. 5 or 10 dollars.

If an insured elects to obtain medical care from a non-network medical provider, the procedure is similar to traditional health insurance in that the insured generally must pay the entire bill up-front and then submit the bill to the insurance carrier for reimbursement of a percentage of the medical bill, e.g., 80%. In addition, the insured may be charged a deductible for non-network medical expenses.

One advantage of a PPO is that the insured is permitted to seek medical care from a specialist without first obtaining permission from a primary physician. The specialist must be a network medical provider. However, preventive medical care may not be covered under a particular PPO plan.

Exclusive Provider Organization (EPO)

Exclusive Provider Organizations are a subset of the PPO with many of the features of the HMO. Under an EPO plan, it is even more costly to obtain medical treatment from a non-network medical provider because the insured is generally responsible for the entire cost without reimbursement.

Point of Service Plan (POS)

A Point of Service plan is similar to a PPO, however, the insured is required to obtain permission from a network primary care physician before seeking treatment from a specialist, even if the specialist is a network provider.

Nevertheless, under a POS plan, the insured still has the right to seek medical care from a non-network medical provider and be entitled to some reimbursement for the cost, although a deductible may apply. If, however, the primary care physician refers the insured to a non-network medical provider, the plan generally pays the costs.

THE CONSOLIDATED OMNIBUS BUDGET RECONCILIATION ACT (COBRA)

Pursuant to the Consolidated Omnibus Budget Reconciliation Act of 1986 (COBRA), employers with 20 or more employees must offer the option of continuation of insurance coverage by the company's group health insurance plan, at the workers' own expense. Under the Act, an employee who is terminated for any reason other than "gross misconduct" is guaranteed the right to continue individual or family health care coverage under the former employer's group plan for as long as 18 months.

The same rule applies if the employee leaves their job voluntarily. In addition, an employee's spouse and dependent children are eligible for COBRA coverage in the event of a divorce or the covered employee's death. However, despite the availability of COBRA health coverage, the costs of obtaining such coverage is quite high because the employee is responsible for paying the entire premium, including administrative costs.

Persons who elect COBRA coverage are generally those who have preexisting conditions, and who are concerned that their health care expenses without coverage will exceed the cost of the premiums. Because the premiums are usually so high, particularly for family coverage, many people take the chance that their health care expenses will be much lower than the cost of COBRA premiums.

Eligibility coverage under the Act also extends to employees in state and local government. Exemptions under the law exist for the District of Columbia, federal employees, and firms employing less than 20 people. In addition, employers with self-funded health plans are exempt from state regulation of their health plans.

Under the Act, employers have to notify employees of their right to COBRA coverage within a certain time period following termination. Employees who wish to elect COBRA coverage must do so within a specified time period.

The health insurance coverage offered under COBRA must be identical to the coverage enjoyed as an employee, although the employee has the right to drop "non-core" benefits such as dental or vision coverage.

Although coverage generally ends after 18 months, certain conditions may qualify the insured for an extension of coverage—e.g., the disability of the former employee—although the premiums may be increased for the additional time period.

MEDICARE

Medicare is a federal health insurance program administered by the Social Security Administration (SSA), designated for seniors and people with disabilities, regardless of income. Medicare was passed into law on July 30, 1965 but beneficiaries were first able to sign-up for the program on July 1, 1966. Medicare is an entitlement program funded by payroll taxes. The Medicare program is administered by private health insurance companies who contract with the federal government to process claims.

Eligibility and Coverage

When a person reaches age 65, he or she usually becomes eligible for Medicare. Unfortunately, Medicare does not cover all health-related expenses, and it is wise to supplement Medicare with additional health insurance coverage.

For example, Medicare does not pay for dentures and routine dental care, eyeglasses, hearing aids, prescription drugs, routine physical checkups, orthopedic devices, and non-skilled nursing home care—items that account for a considerable portion of medical expenses, particularly for senior citizens.

As set forth below, there are two parts to the Medicare policy: (i) Part A Hospitalization Coverage; and (ii) Part B Medical Coverage.

Part A Hospitalization Coverage

Part A is hospital insurance that covers hospital care as well as skilled nursing facility, hospice and home health care. Under Part A, there is a designated deductible—i.e., an initial amount one must pay for their hospitalization before Medicare begins to pay any additional expenses. This amount—known as the hospital deductible—increases every January 1st.

Medicare Part A benefits are free to most people 65 and older. In general, anyone eligible for Social Security or Railroad Retirement Benefits are also eligible for free Part A benefits. Persons who have been receiving Social Security disability benefits for a period of 24 months also qualify for Part A hospital coverage. Others may be eligible for Medicare if they pay a monthly premium.

If an individual has enrolled in Medicare and is also working and covered under their employer's group health plan, Medicare is still the primary payer if the employer has less than 20 employees. Medicare is the secondary payer if the employer has 20 or more employees and provides group health insurance. However, because Medicare Part A is free, an eligible individual should sign up for Part A once they are eligible, whether or not they have other insurance.

Eligible persons receive a health insurance card, known as a Medicare card, to claim their benefits. Persons already receiving Social Security automatically receive Medicare cards as part of their Social Security benefits.

Under Part A, the duration of care per benefit period is limited. A *benefit period* begins when the patient first enters a hospital or other facility, and ends after he or she has been discharged from the facility for a continuous period of at least 60 days from the date of discharge. This rule is simply a measurement device. There is no limit to the number of periods in which one may receive benefits. The benefit periods depend on the type of care received, as follows:

Hospital Care

Part A entitles the patient to 90 days of in-hospital care for each *benefit period*. There is a deductible for each benefit period. In addition, the patient has to pay a *co-insurance amount* for days 61 through 90. After the patient has exhausted their 90 days of coverage, Medicare will pay for an additional 60 days of care during the patient's lifetime. The patient will have to pay a portion during these "reserve" days. Additional coverage may be obtained through the purchase of a MediGap policy, which is further discussed below.

Hospitals cannot refuse patients on the ground that their health coverage is through Part A of Medicare. Remember, though, not all hospital stays or services are covered by Medicare. It is the hospital's responsibility to inform you if something is not covered.

Skilled Nursing Facility Benefits

Part A entitles the patient to 100 days of care in a Medicare-certified skilled nursing facility (SNF) per benefit period, provided: (i) the patient was hospitalized for at least three days during the 30 days prior to admission in the SNF and (ii) the patient needs and receives daily skilled services. Medicare defines "daily" as seven days a week of skilled nursing and five days a week of skilled therapy. Skilled nursing and therapy services include evaluation and management as well as observation and assessment of a patient's condition. Medicare pays for the first 20 days in full. For days 21 through 100, the patient pays a portion of the costs.

Home Health Care Benefits

Medicare Part A covers up to 35 hours a week of home health aide and *skilled nursing services* if a patient is homebound and requires skilled services on an *intermittent* basis. *Skilled nursing services* include the administration of medication, tube feedings, catheter changes and wound care. *Intermittent* usually means less than five days per week, but some people who receive home health care services up to seven days a week will be covered if the services are only needed for a finite and predictable amount of time. A patient can also qualify for up to 35 hours per week of home health aide services if they are homebound and need skilled physical, speech or occupational therapy.

To be covered, the patient must receive services from a Medicare-certified Home Health Agency (CHHA). Medicare home health coverage is available indefinitely so long as the patient remains homebound and continues to require skilled nursing services on an intermittent basis or skilled therapy services.

There is no prior hospitalization requirement and the benefit covers individuals with chronic illnesses as well as those who are acutely ill. The benefit is available at no cost to the patient, and there is no deductible or co-insurance required.

Hospice Benefits

Under Part A, hospice benefits are available to terminally ill patients. Medicare will cover 95 percent of the cost of hospice care, and the patient will have to pay the remaining five percent. Once the patient elects Medicare hospice benefits, he or she becomes ineligible to receive benefits for hospital care related to the terminal illness.

Part B Medical Coverage

Part B of the medicare policy covers most reasonable and necessary health-related expenses, other than hospitalization, including certain physician services, therapy services, outpatient hospital care, laboratory and diagnostic tests, supplies, durable medical equipment such as a wheelchair, and many other specified medical expenses not covered by Part A. Medicare sets approved charges for all of the medical services it covers.

Medicare does not cover many common health expenses, such as prescription drugs, routine checkups, vision and hearing care, custodial care, or dental care. It also does not cover experimental procedures.

In 1997, Congress passed a law which set forth new covered preventive care services at no extra cost, including: (i) yearly mammograms; (ii) pap smears including pelvic and breast examinations; (iii) colorectal cancer screening; (iv) bone mass measurement; (v) flu and pneumococcal pneumonia shots; and (vi) diabetes glucose monitoring and diabetes education for individuals with diabetes.

Anyone who is eligible for Part A hospital coverage is eligible for Part B medical coverage, however, Part B is not free. There is a monthly premium that increases every January 1st.

Part B medical coverage, unlike Part A, is based on a calendar year, rather than on benefit periods. The Part B medical coverage yearly deductible is $100.00 dollars. After the deductible is paid, Medicare pays 80% percent of the approved reasonable charges for covered services for the balance of the year.

Unfortunately, many health care providers charge substantially more than Medicare's approved charge for their services, and the patient must pay for any charges that are above the approved Medicare rate. For example, there is no limit on what ambulance companies and durable medical equipment suppliers may charge. The Medicare-approved portion may represent only a small part of the total bill.

Some health care providers, however, "take assignment," which means that they agree to accept Medicare's approved charge as payment in full. Medicare pays 80% of the approved charge, and the patient pays the remaining twenty percent. The local Medicare carrier has a directory that lists all doctors and suppliers in a particular area who always take assignment. To limit the amount one pays for medical expenses, it is a good idea to obtain a copy of this directory and use it when choosing health care providers.

When doctors don't "take assignment," federal law limits the amount that they may charge Medicare patients to 15% above Medicare's approved charge. Some states, including Massachusetts, Minnesota, Rhode Island, Pennsylvania, Ohio, Connecticut, Vermont and New York, have even stricter limits.

If an individual waits to enroll in Part B until he or she is older than 65, their monthly premium may be higher, since Medicare imposes a ten percent premium penalty for every year enrollment is delayed. However, if an individual is working and covered under their employer's group health plan, they may delay enrolling without a penalty until seven months after retirement.

However, it may not be cost-effective to sign up for Part B if you are already covered under an employer group health plan. That's because you will have to pay Medicare's Part B monthly premium and annual deductible, and your returns will be limited. In addition, it may be wise to stay in your employer's health plan after retirement, if that is an option, since any new insurance plans, including Medigap, may exclude pre-existing health problems for up to six months.

Denial of Medicare Claims

Under Medicare Part A hospital coverage, if a Medicare claim is denied, the hospital or Medicare review board must inform the claimant in writing if their stay will not—or will no longer—be covered by Medicare. The denial notice will set forth the procedures to follow in order to have the denial reconsidered. Many such denials are overturned.

If, after reconsideration, the claimant is still not satisfied, there are further remedies for appealing the decision. A large number of appeals are successful.

Under Medicare Part B coverage, if a claim is denied, the claimant will receive an "Explanation of Medicare Benefits." The claimant then has six months to ask for the denial to be reconsidered and overturned. If the claim is again rejected, the claimant has an additional six months to request a hearing through their local Medicare carrier. If the claim is again denied, the claimant has 60 days to request a hearing before an administrative law judge.

Medicare + Choice

In 1997, Congress passed a law which made many changes in the Medicare program, including a new section known as *Medicare + Choice*, which creates new health plan options for Medicare recipients.

Under the new law, a Medicare recipient can decide to: (i) continue receiving Medicare benefits under the original Medicare plan, (ii) continue receiving Medicare benefits under the original Medicare plan supplemented by one of ten available Medigap insurance policies, as further discussed below; or (iii) change to a plan that gives them at least the same, and possibly more, benefits than under the original Medicare plan.

There are differences among the new health plans including: (i) the cost; (ii) the availability of extra benefits; and (iii) the participant's choice in using certain doctors, hospitals and other medical providers.

In order to be eligible for Medicare + Choice, a recipient must have Medicare Parts A and B, and not have permanent kidney failure. Nevertheless, no matter which health plan option one chooses, they are still in the Medicare program and are still entitled to all of the services Medicare covers.

A Medicare Patient's Statement of Rights is set forth at Appendix 11.

Additional health care options available under the Medicare + Choice program include:

Medicare Managed Care Plan

A Medicare managed care plan is a Medicare approved network of doctors, hospitals, and other health care providers that agrees to give care in return for a set monthly payment from Medicare. Some managed care plans may provide extra benefits, and some may charge the participant a premium.

A managed care plan may be any of the following: (i) A Health Maintenance Organization (HMO); (ii) Provider Sponsored Organization (PSO); Preferred Provider Organization (PPO); or a Health Maintenance Organization with a Point of Service Option (POS).

An HMO or PSO usually asks the participant to use only the doctors and hospitals in the plan's network. If so, there are little or no out-of-pocket cost for covered services. A PPO or POS usually lets the participant use doctors and hospitals outside of the plan for an extra out-of-pocket cost.

Private Fee-for-Service Plan (PFFS)

A private fee-for-service plan (PFFS) is a Medicare-approved private insurance plan. Medicare pays the plan a premium for Medicare-covered services. A PFFS Plan provides all Medicare benefits. A PFFS Plan is not the same as a Medigap policy.

The PFFS Plan, rather than Medicare, decides how much to pay for the covered services the participant receives. Providers may bill the participant more than the plan pays, up to a limit, and the participant must pay the difference. It is likely that the participant will pay a premium for a PFFS plan.

Medicare Medical Savings Account Plan (MSA)

A Medicare medical savings account plan (MSA) is a health insurance policy with a high yearly deductible. This is a test program for up to 390,000 Medicare beneficiaries. Medicare pays the premium for the Medicare MSA Plan and deposits money into a separate Medicare MSA established by the participant. The participant uses the money in the Medicare MSA to pay for medical expenses.

The participant can accumulate money in their Medicare MSA to pay for extra medical costs. The insurance policy has a high deductible and there are no limits on what providers can charge above what is paid by the Medicare MSA Plan. A participant can only enroll in a Medicare MSA

Plan during the month of November, and must remain in the plan for a full year.

Further information about the Medicare + Choice program may be obtained from the State Health Insurance Assistance Program in an individual's area. The State Health Insurance Assistance Program will help an individual with Medicare questions or provide information about other available health care options.

PRESCRIPTION DRUG LEGISLATION

Legislation has been proposed which would allow Medicare beneficiaries to buy prescription drugs at a reduced cost. Studies show that drug price discrimination hits hardest at those who need medicines the most. Numerous state studies demonstrate that pharmaceutical manufacturers charge seniors up to twice as much as most favored customers, such as the Departments of Defense and Veterans Affairs.

Seniors are 12% of the population but use 37% of prescription drugs. The average senior fills 18 prescriptions a year. Seniors now pay more for prescription drugs than any other medical expenditure except physician services. One in eight senior citizens has had to choose between purchasing food and prescription drugs, according to the Senate Special Committee on Aging.

Under the Prescription Drug Fairness for Seniors Act (H.R. 664/S. 731), Medicare recipients would be able to purchase prescription drugs up to 40% off current retail prices.

As of May 25, 2000 153 House members and 12 Senators have co-sponsored the Act, making it the most broadly supported drug reform bill in Congress. Its chief House and Senate sponsors are Rep. Tom Allen (D-Maine) and Sen. Tim Johnson (D-S.D.). The Allen-Johnson legislation would end price discrimination by prescription drug makers against senior citizens and the disabled on Medicare who have no or inadequate prescription drug insurance coverage.

The Act requires prescription drug makers to provide them with their "best" prices. Pharmacies would purchase prescription drugs for Medicare beneficiaries from the manufacturer at the same low prices available to the federal government and other large purchasers. Since these prices are about 40% less than the retail prices paid by Medicare beneficiaries, seniors will be able to benefit from large cost savings.

The text of The Prescription Drug Fairness for Seniors Act is set forth at Appendix 12.

Senior citizens wishing to contact their government representatives in connection with the prescription drug initiatives or other initiatives of interest to the elder population can contact the Congressional Committees on Aging at the following addresses:

The House of Representatives

House Select Committee on Aging
712 House Office Building, Annex #1
Washington, DC 20515-6361
Tel: 202-226-3375

The Senate

Senate Special Committee on Aging
Dirksen Senate Office Building, Room SD-G41
Washington, DC 20510-6400
Tel: 202-224-5364

SUPPLEMENTAL HEALTH INSURANCE PROGRAMS

Medigap Insurance

Medicare does not pay for all of an individual's medical expenses. Therefore, eligible Medicare recipients may also purchase supplemental coverage known as Medigap insurance. Medigap policies generally pay for medical-related expenses not reimbursed by Medicare, such as hospital deductibles and co-payments.

Medigap policies are designed to supplement Medicare and generally do not cover long-term care, although some policies do provide for skilled nursing home care and at-home recovery care. There are ten variations of Medigap plans available through private insurance companies. The basic benefits offered under all plans include:

1. Hospital co-insurance;

2. Full coverage for 365 additional hospital days to be used after exhaustion of Medicare hospital reserve days;

3. Twenty percent co-payment for physician and other Part B services; and

4. Three pints of blood.

There are a number of additional benefits available depending upon the plan you select. These benefits include:

1. Coverage of the Medicare hospital deductible;

2. Skilled nursing facility daily co-insurance;

3. Coverage of the Part B $100 deductible;

4. Eighty percent of emergency medical costs outside the U.S. during the first two months of a trip;

5. Payment to cover the difference when a doctor's fees are over the Medicare-approved charge;

6. At-home custodial care in addition to and in conjunction with Medicare-approved home care;

7. Some prescription drug coverage; and

8. Some preventive medical care coverage.

There are many services a Medigap plan will not cover. These include:

1. Custodial care—such as feeding, bathing and grooming—either at home or in a nursing home;

2. Long-term skilled care in a nursing home;

3. Unlimited prescription drugs;

4. Vision care;

5. Dental care; or

6. Private nurses.

In addition, if Medicare refuses to cover medical care because it is unreasonable and unnecessary or experimental, Medigap will not cover it either.

Once you select a Medigap policy, you have 30 days to review the plan and cancel it without penalty. You also are allowed to change or cancel your policy once a year, although in most states your insurer can reject your application for more comprehensive coverage. However, if you wish to downgrade your policy, you may do so.

If an individual does opt to enroll in a Medigap plan, it's usually best to do so during the six months following enrollment in Medicare Part B. During that period, insurance companies must let the insured sign up for the plan of their choice, without regard to health or age.

Further information concerning Medigap insurance policies may be obtained from the National Insurance Consumer Helpline at (800) 942-4242.

The Qualified Medicare Beneficiary Program

Persons who receive Medicare and have income and resources below a certain amount may be eligible for the Qualified Medicare Beneficiary (QMB) program. Under the QMB program, the State pays Medicare premiums, deductibles and coinsurance for persons who qualify for the program

Medicaid

Medicaid is a government program designed to provide health services, including nursing home care, to persons who are financially eligible. Medicaid eligibility is determined by a number of factors, the most important of which is income level.

Only certain classes of individuals are eligible for Medicaid, including: (i) elderly persons who, although eligible for Medicare, cannot afford it; (ii) disabled persons; (iii) pregnant women; and (iv) children from low-income households.

Each state formulates and administers its own Medicaid program, following federal government guidelines, through matching federal funds based on the state's per capita income. Within these guidelines, states have considerable freedom in managing their own Medicaid program, thus coverage varies from state-to-state. For example, individual states set the financial eligibility criteria for Medicaid in their jurisdiction, often well below federally established poverty levels.

Medicaid offers more comprehensive coverage than Medicare. However, the program's low reimbursement levels discourages private medical providers from participating in the program.

Medicaid pays for costs not covered by Medicare for elderly persons who qualify for Medicare but cannot afford the Part A hospital deductible or Part B premium. Nevertheless, Medicaid is generally not an alternative resource to most persons in need of long-term care because of the stringent restrictions. To be eligible for Medicaid, one must first exhaust all of their assets and savings—not including their home—a process known as "spending down."

An exception exists under the spouse impoverishment provisions of Medicare, which provide that the spouse of a person receiving long-term care in a nursing home is permitted to keep a certain dollar amount of assets and income, and still be eligible for Medicaid. However, the amount one is allowed to retain is still very modest.

Older Americans Act

Under the *Older Americans Act of 1965*, states are allocated federal funds for the purpose of setting up agencies designed to provide services to persons over the age of 60. Unfortunately, these services are limited in scope, subject to eligibility standards, and not available in all areas. Services provided under this statute may include home health care, adult day care, homemaker services, transportation, and meal delivery programs.

Social Services Block Grants (Title XX)

The Social Services Block Grants program, established under Title XX of the Social Security Act provides for allocation of federal funds to the states to assist low-income persons with non-medical daily living services, such as those provided under the Older Americans Act. These services are also not widely available and thus may not be an option for most persons.

Anyone over 65 who is eligible for Social Security or Railroad Retirement Benefits—a program similar to Social Security for railroad employees, their spouses and survivors—is automatically eligible. People with disabilities who have received Social Security Disability Income for at least 24 months and some people who are receiving regular dialysis or have received a kidney transplant because of kidney failure are also automatically eligible. U. S. citizens are automatically eligible as are permanent legal residents who have been continuously residing in the United States for at least five years, though they must file an application.

LONG-TERM HEALTH CARE

In General

Many senior citizens are able to live out their lives independently and in good health. Unfortunately, many others have health care problems which render them feeble and dependent on others to help them with their daily activities.

Unlike acute care—short-term, recuperative care provided by a hospital—long-term care is the type of care given to persons who have become disabled or who suffer from a chronic illness. In such a case, important decisions must be made about the proper setting in which such care may be given.

Nursing Homes

Often, the decision is made to place a dependent senior citizen in a nursing home. This decision raises a number of difficult issues, such as whether a nursing home is affordable, and whether it is a suitable placement for the senior citizen. The term nursing home generally refers to a residential facility that provides shelter and care for senior citizens who are unable to live independently. Federal law guarantees nursing home residents certain rights, applicable whether it is publicly or privately owned institution. These rights include, but are not limited to:

(1) the right to be free from physical or mental harm or abuse;

(2) the right to privacy; and

(3) the right to choose your own physician and participate in your health care decisions.

The State Offices of Long-Term Care Ombudsman are agencies actively involved with nursing homes in an effort to improve the conditions for senior citizens.

A Directory of the State Offices of Long-Term Care Ombudsman is set forth at Appendix 13.

Types of Nursing Homes

In general, there are three types of nursing homes:

Personal Care Nursing Facility

A Personal Care Nursing Facility provides the senior citizen who does not need any special medical care with room and board and basic assistance with daily activities. Medicare and Medicaid generally does not pay for this type of long-term care.

Medicaid Nursing Facility

A Medicaid Nursing Facility provides the senior citizen with a limited range of skilled nursing care, rehabilitation services, and other necessary health-related care. Medicare does not pay for residence in such facilities, however Medicaid may reimburse the costs of such care provided a doctor certifies that the senior citizen is in need of this level of care. Further, the resident must meet certain financial guidelines to qualify for admission.

Medicare Skilled Nursing Facility (SNF)

A Medicare Skilled Nursing Facility provides the senior citizen with the most highly skilled nursing care available outside of a hospital setting, including many specialized services. Medicare pays up to 150 days per calendar year for residence at such a facility, provided your physician certifies that you are in need of such a high level of care.

Long-Term Health Care Insurance

Unfortunately, nursing home care is extremely expensive, and is rarely covered by private health insurance. If a senior citizen doesn't qualify under the Medicare or Medicaid programs, he or she must finance their own care. The majority of the cost of this care is borne by the patients and their families. This is particularly burdensome in the retirement years when most older persons are on fixed incomes.

Responding to the need for financial assistance in the event long-term care becomes necessary, a large number of insurance companies have stepped in to fill the gap, providing a variety of insurance policies covering long-term care. If one is considering purchasing such a policy, it would be prudent to review the benefits being offered by the various companies in order to choose the policy that best fits your needs.

With the exception of the Medicaid program, which has limited eligibility, much of what is covered under long-term health care insurance is either not covered at all, or only partially covered under Medicare or private health insurance policies. The cost of fully providing such care would be prohibitive. The average cost of care in a nursing home is estimated at $25,000 per year and more, depending on the facility, the location, and the level of care provided. Home care costs can range from $50 to $200 per day, again depending on the level of care and the number of hours provided.

Although long-term care insurance can be very helpful if it is ever needed, it can also be quite costly, ranging anywhere from $250 to over $2000 per year for the average senior citizen who is in good health. Before taking on this considerable expense, it would be wise to carefully assess one's individual situation and investigate all resources available from other programs. Some of the factors one should consider when assessing the need for long-term care insurance, include:

1. The individual's present financial situation and projected financial situation following retirement.

2. The individual's ability to afford long-term care insurance.

3. The programs the individual expects to be eligible for upon retirement and whether they will be able to meet his or her needs.

4. The likelihood that the individual will require long-term care in the future, based on his or her present health and family history.

5. The alternative resources the individual expects to have if long-term care is needed, such as family and friends, and the availability of community-based services.

Choosing a Long-Term Care Insurance Policy

Since long-term care insurance is a fairly recent development, one must be very careful in selecting and evaluating the various policies available, and inquiring into the background and stability of the companies offering such insurance.

Every policy generally contains some restrictions and limitations, and some policies may not be available due to such factors as age and health. Carefully read all of the provisions of the policy before making your decision. If any of the provisions are unclear, you should seek professional assistance in understanding the policy. In general, the policy should be flexible enough to cover all levels of nursing home and home health care without undue restrictions, such as stipulations as to the facilities at which the individual can receive care. In addition, the policy should have a renewal guarantee.

Typical Long-Term Care Insurance Provisions

Although the provisions, limitations and restrictions of long-term care insurance policies may vary, there are a number of typical provisions found in most policies. Some of these provisions are discussed below.

Coverage

Long-term care insurance policies typically cover nursing home care. Some policies cover all levels of nursing home care—skilled nursing care, intermediate care, and custodial care—while others may cover only a certain level of care, such as skilled nursing care. It is best to purchase a policy that covers all levels of nursing home care, since long-term skilled nursing care is not usually needed. It is more likely that a person will need a lesser level of nursing home care, such as custodial care, over an extended period of time. Also be aware of any limitations or prerequisites to such care.

Home health care is generally provided for in long-term care insurance policies. Again, however, one must be aware of any limitations on the availability of such care. For example, some policies may only provide home health care after hospitalization, which may not be necessary in every case even though the individual may be in need of home health care services. In addition, long-term care insurance may include coverage for such services as assistance with household chores, shopping, transportation and personal hygiene, as well as long-term skilled nursing care.

Benefits

Most policies pay only a preset daily benefit for nursing home care or home health care, and the difference between the amount covered by the insurance and the actual costs of care is borne by the insured. Some policies allow the insured to pay higher premiums in return for higher daily benefits. When considering inflation, one must be aware that in many cases the benefits payable under the policy will not be increased. Therefore, the individual will be responsible for any escalation in the costs of care due to inflation.

To avoid this problem, one must shop around for a policy that provides for benefit increases over time due to inflation. One must also be aware of any limits the policy places on the duration of care and the benefits payable under the policy. Generally, policies that provide for a longer duration of care and benefits will be more costly.

Policy Restrictions

Most long-term care policies contain various restrictions. For example, a restriction on preexisting conditions—conditions that existed prior to the policy's effective date—typically denies the insured any benefits connected with those specific health conditions for a designated waiting period after the effective date of the policy.

Another restriction that often appears in long-term care insurance policies is the waiting period, known as the elimination period, during which the policy does not pay benefits. For example, if a policy specifies that benefits for home health care will begin on the 21st day, that means the insured is responsible for payment out-of-pocket for the first 20 days of home health care. Lower cost policies may contain waiting periods that are considerably longer. In considering a policy's waiting periods, you must determine whether it is worth the higher premium to insure that you will receive benefits at the earliest possible date.

Eligibility coverage under the Act also extends to employees in state and local government. Exemptions under the law exist for the District of Columbia, federal employees, and firms employing less than 20 people. In addition, employers with self-funded health plans are exempt from state regulation of their health plans.

Under the Act, employers have to notify employees of their right to CO-BRA coverage within a certain time period following termination. Employees who wish to elect COBRA coverage must do so within a specified time period.

The health insurance coverage offered under COBRA must be identical to the coverage enjoyed as an employee, although the employee has the right to drop "non-core" benefits such as dental or vision coverage.

Although coverage generally ends after 18 months, certain conditions may qualify the insured for an extension of coverage—e.g., the disability of the former employee—although the premiums may be increased for the additional time period.

CHAPTER 4:
ADVANCE DIRECTIVES

IN GENERAL

Advance directives are the instructions one prepares in order to designate his or her wishes concerning end-of-life health care treatment. Executing an advance directive gives an individual the opportunity to make his or her own health care decisions long after he or she has lost the capacity to do so. The opportunity to execute advance directives responds to the individual's wishes to have some control over his or her destiny. Advance directives respond to the individual's fear that medical technology will prolong their life long after any reasonable possibility of recovery has disappeared.

Many people prefer to "die with dignity" rather than remain comatose in a hospital bed attached to life support equipment for an indefinite duration. Further, the emotional toll that such a scenario causes the patient's family is another important factor to be considered. An advance directive authorizes the medical care provider to cease some or all of these life support measures. On the other hand, an advance directive may also be used to instruct the medical care provider to undertake certain life-sustaining treatments in certain defined circumstances. In short, it is about giving the patient the choice and the right to make these decisions.

TYPES OF ADVANCED DIRECTIVES

An "Advance directive" is a general term that refers to one's oral and written instructions about their future medical care, in the event that they become unconscious or too sick to express their intentions. However, as long as the patient is able to express their own decisions, an advance directive will not be used and the patient can accept or refuse any medical treatment regardless of the advance directive.

In general, there are two types of advance directives: (1) A Living Will; and (2) A Durable Power of Attorney for Health Care. However, if you execute both a Living Will and a Durable Power of Attorney for Health

Care, you must make sure that the terms of both documents are consistent to avoid confusion or invalidation. Discuss this matter with your physician and provide a copy of your documents.

It is important to check with your hospital to make sure your documents conform to their requirements. If your physician, or your hospital, appear to be unwilling to comply with your wishes, you should consider finding alternative medical care.

Discuss this matter with your family, so that they will be prepared if called on to support your decision. Provide copies of your living will and durable power of attorney documents to your family and your minister, rabbi, or other religious advisor. Do not keep your living will or power of attorney in a place where they will not be easily found. You must make your wishes known ahead of time to ensure that they will be followed. An advance directive may be amended or revoked at the will of the individual executing the directive.

All 50 states and the District of Columbia have laws recognizing the use of advance directives. The availability and scope of one or both advance directives varies from state to state, therefore, the reader is advised to check the law of his or her jurisdiction for specific provisions.

THE LIVING WILL

A living will is a written declaration, directed to your physician, stating that you wish to forgo extraordinary treatment of a terminal illness, in order to die a natural death. Although living wills may not be statutorily recognized in all states, the majority of states have enacted "right to die" legislation. Further, an individual has a constitutional right to execute a living will.

The purpose of right-to-die legislation is to give a person some say over the manner in which they will be treated should they develop an incurable illness or enter a persistent vegetative state, and become unable to communicate their wishes at that time.

A living will provides family and loved ones some guidance in making a very painful decision. It also allows health care providers to withdraw or withhold life-support treatment without risking a medical malpractice lawsuit. Generally, a living will provides that no heroic measures should be taken to prolong the individual's life where there is no reasonable expectation of recovery. However, pain medication is still usually administered.

A sample Living Will is set forth at Appendix 14.

Requirements

There are certain requirements that must be met to ensure recognition of a living will, and some states require the use of a statutory form for a living will to be valid. Although state laws vary, right to die statutes generally require that there be two witnesses to the maker's signature, neither of whom can be related to the maker or beneficiaries of his or her estate. In addition, two physicians must diagnose the patient as terminally ill. Many states also provide that a living will is valid only if signed after the physician has informed the patient that he or she has an incurable illness. Before executing a living will, it is prudent to determine exactly what requirements are imposed in your state.

A table of state Living Will statutes is set forth at Appendix 15.

Durable Power of Attorney for Health Care

In order to have your wishes concerning medical treatment known and honored should you become incapacitated, you can designate a health care agent by executing what is generally known as a Durable Power of Attorney for Health Care, also known as a Health Care Proxy in some jurisdictions. In effect, the person you appoint "stands in your shoes" for the purposes of making your health care decisions.

You can specify the type of treatment you desire, as well as the type of treatment you do not want. For example, you can instruct your "attorney-in-fact" to either require or prohibit the use of life-support systems should you be diagnosed with a terminal illness, or you can leave that decision in his or her hands.

A sample Durable Power of Attorney for Health Care is set forth in the Appendix 16.

WITHDRAWAL OF OR WITHHOLDING MEDICAL TREATMENT

An individual has a constitutional right to request the withdrawal or withholding of medical treatment, including the cessation of food and water, even if doing so will result in the person's death. Honoring a person's right to refuse medical treatment or other life sustaining intervention, especially at the end of life, is the most widely practiced and widely accepted right to die policy in our society.

Patients have the right to stop not only commonly recognized life support measures, such as respirators, but to also discontinue any other medical treatments that may prolong life, such as kidney dialysis, heart medication, antibiotics, blood transfusions, etc., regardless of whether the refusal may result in death. Nevertheless, the patient is also entitled to receive symptomatic treatment, such as pain medication, even if the pain medication has the effect of hastening their death.

Under the law, a health care provider cannot commence a medical procedure without first obtaining a patient's informed consent. Thus, a health care provider who imposes medical treatment contrary to the instructions left in an advance directive may be guilty of medical battery. Claims of battery against physicians for nonconsensual medical care have been recognized for some time even if the medical procedure is harmless, beneficial, or life-sustaining. The courts are becoming increasingly willing to find that battery has occurred in cases in which a health care provider refused to honor the directions left in an advance directive or given by an appointed agent.

The *Cruzan* Decision

The *Cruzan* case involved a petition brought by parents to remove life support from their daughter who was in a persistent vegetative state. The holding in *Cruzan* supports the desirability of individual choice in the formalization of advance directives.

In *Cruzan*, the Supreme Court held that:

1. Patients have the right to reject treatment, including life-sustaining treatment;

2. There is no distinction between artificial hydration and nutrition and any other form of treatment;

3. The distinction between "withholding" and "withdrawing" treatment is of no significance; and

4. The present incompetence of the patient is not an essential barrier to respecting the patient's wishes.

Nevertheless, the Supreme Court affirmed the individual state's right to set their own standards concerning evidence of an incompetent patient's wishes. By implication, this means that the state is not bound to honor the wishes of family members of the patient, but can set forth its own criteria to follow.

For example, the state may require (1) an explicit statement by the patient as to his or her wishes concerning the withholding of certain treatment, i.e. the execution of a "living will" or (2) the appointment by the patient of a proxy to make those decisions in the event of his or her incapacitation, i.e., the "durable power of attorney for health care.

In the *Cruzan* case, the State of Missouri required "clear and convincing evidence" that Ms. Cruzan wished to have life-sustaining treatment withheld, in this case tubal feeding.

The Supreme Court decision effectively permitted the state of Missouri to reject the petition brought by the parents. However, if Ms. Cruzan had executed advance directives which set forth her wishes to have treatment withheld, or if she had appointed a proxy to make those decisions on her behalf, the Supreme Court would have upheld her wishes according to her constitutional right.

DO NOT RESUSCITATE ORDERS

A "do not resuscitate" order (DNR) refers to instructions given by the patient, or the patient's authorized representative, which generally provide that the patient does not want the medical staff to attempt cardiopulmonary resuscitation (CPR) in the event he or she suffers cardiac or respiratory arrest.

Prior to issuing a DNR order, the patient's attending physician must provide certain information to the patient, or to the surrogate, concerning the patient's condition, including:

1. The patient's diagnosis and prognosis;

2. The reasonably foreseeable risks and benefits of CPR; and

3. The consequences of a DNR order.

If the attending physician objects to the issuance of a DNR order, he or she must inform the patient or surrogate of that objection, and make arrangements to transfer the patient to another physician who will comply with the patient's directive.

ASSISTED SUICIDE

Assisted suicide refers to the ending of one's life with the help of another, usually a physician. Unlike advance directives, which are passive in nature, assisted suicide actively hastens death. Assisted suicide has also been referred to as mercy killing or active euthanasia. Although society at one time shunned the concept of assisted suicide and likened it to murder, the development of the law in this area seems to show that assisted suicide is gaining acceptance.

Euthanasia, translated literally, simply means a "good death." The term has traditionally been used to refer to the hastening of a suffering person's death or "mercy killing," and it may be voluntary or involuntary. Involuntary active euthanasia is one of the least accepted social policies. It refers to an intervention that ends a patient's life without obtaining the informed consent of the patient. Voluntary active euthanasia involves an intervention requested by a competent individual that is administered to cause death, such as a lethal injection. Although no law currently authorizes this practice, polls show that a growing number of Americans support honoring a patient's request for voluntary active euthanasia. Assisted suicide has been the subject of intense national debate.

In June, 1997 the U.S. Supreme Court handed down decisions in two cases challenging the legality of state bans on assisted suicide. In both cases the Court found that there was no constitutional right to assisted suicide and turned the matter back to states to decide whether to ban or legalize assisted suicide. Oregon became the first state to permit physician-assisted suicide in limited circumstances when it enacted the Oregon Death With Dignity Act in 1994. The Act was not implemented due to court challenges until 1997 when the voters refused to repeal the Act by an overwhelming majority. A number of states have proposed similar legislation.

Proponents of assisted suicide see the request for assistance in dying as an extension of an individual's right to control over their end-of-life health care decisions. Opponents to the procedure fear that the "right-to-die" may eventually turn into a coercive "duty-to-die" targeted at the elderly or infirm.

A directory of national organizations supporting choice-in-dying is set forth at Appendix 17.

CHAPTER 5:
AGE DISCRIMINATION

IN GENERAL

There are federal and state laws in place which protect the senior citizen from discrimination based on their age. As further discussed below, these laws extend to, among other areas, employment, housing and the granting of consumer credit.

EMPLOYMENT

The Age Discrimination in Employment Act of 1967

Age discrimination in employment is governed by the Age Discrimination in Employment Act of 1967 (the "ADEA"), as amended. The ADEA prohibits employment discrimination against individuals 40 years of age and older. The United States Equal Employment Opportunity Commission (EEOC) is an independent federal agency established by Congress in 1964 to enforce Title VII of the Civil Rights Act of 1964 and other federal laws aimed at eradicating discrimination in employment.

The ADEA pertains to federal, state and local employers, as well as private employers provided they employ 20 or more employees. Unions and employment agencies are also subject to the ADEA provided they meet certain criteria.

The ADEA prohibits age discrimination in all aspects of employment, such as hiring decisions, advancement opportunities, compensation and termination. Mandatory retirement is prohibited under the ADEA except in certain limited situations.

Additional remedies may be available under state anti-discrimination laws, which may also apply in situations where the ADEA does not, e.g. in the case of employers of less than 20 employees.

Employees seeking to bring a claim under the ADEA must file a claim with the EEOC within 180 days of the discriminatory act. Some states require that the employee first file their claim with the state's own equal employment opportunity or state human resources agency. These states are known as deferral states which elect to make their own investigation prior to that of the EEOC.

In deferral states, the EEOC's 180 day time limitation is extended to 300 days after the discriminatory act, or 30 days after notice that the state has terminated its proceedings. The employee is entitled to bring a private civil suit in state or federal court against the employer 60 days after filing the complaint with the EEOC or state agency. This may be done even though the EEOC or state agency has not completed its investigation. If, however, the EEOC files a lawsuit based on its investigation, it preempts any lawsuit brought by the employee. Under the statute, a lawsuit must be brought within 2 years of the discriminatory act, or 3 years if the act was willful.

In order to prevail in an age discrimination lawsuit, the employee has the burden of proving a prima facie case, which includes a showing that the employee is: (1) a member of the protected class, i.e. over 40; (2) adversely affected by the employer's action; and that (3) age was the determining factor in the employer's action. Once a prima facie case has been demonstrated, the employer has the burden of showing that the action was taken for some legitimate nondiscriminatory reason.

If the employer is able to do so, the burden shifts again to the employee to show that the stated reason is merely a pretext. If the employee prevails, he or she may be entitled to a money damage award, and equitable relief, e.g. reinstatement.

Filing the Discrimination Charge With the EEOC

Discrimination charges may be filed in person, by mail, or by telephone. The EEOC is headquartered in Washington, D.C., and operates 50 field offices throughout the United States. Individuals seeking to file a charge may contact their nearest EEOC field office, or contact EEOC headquarters at (TEL:) 800-669-4000/(TDD): 800-669-6820 for further instructions on filing the charge. If an individual is going to need some type of special assistance in filing the charge, such as an interpreter, they should give the EEOC advance notice of such need.

In filing a discrimination charge, the charging party will be required to supply the EEOC with the following information:

1. The charging party's name, address and telephone number;

2. The name, address, and telephone number of the respondent employer, employment agency, or union that is alleged to have discriminated, and the number of employees or union members, if known;

3. A short description of the discriminatory act which is alleged to have violated the law;

4. The date of the alleged violation.

Among the EEOC's recent litigation achievements are:

1. A $13 million back pay settlement in an age bias case against Lockheed Martin (formerly Martin Marietta), which also included reinstatement of 450 jobs for older workers who were dismissed.

CONSUMER CREDIT

The Equal Credit Opportunity Act (ECOA)

In the past, many older persons complained about being denied credit just because they were over a certain age. When they retired, they often found their credit suddenly cut off or reduced. Senior citizens are now protected from discrimination in the granting of credit on the basis of age. Such discriminatory practices were made illegal by the passage of the Equal Credit Opportunity Act (ECOA) and Federal Reserve Regulation B, the regulation which interprets the ECOA.

The ECOA is an attempt to assure that credit granting decisions are based solely on business judgment and repayment capacity. Under the ECOA, those who grant consumer credit are prohibited from discriminating in the granting of credit based on sex, marital status, race, color, religion, national origin, receipt of public assistance benefits, and age.

The law is very specific about how a person's age may be used in credit decisions. A creditor may ask your age, but if you're old enough to sign a binding contract, a creditor may not:

1. Turn you down, offer you less credit, or offer you less favorable credit terms because of your age;

2. Ignore your retirement income in evaluating your application;

3. Close your credit account or require you to reapply for it just because you reach a certain age or retire; or

4. Deny you credit or close your account because credit life insurance or other credit-related insurance is not available to persons your age.

Violation of the law may result in an award of actual damages, including legal costs and fees, and subject the creditor to a punitive damage award up to $10,000.

Nevertheless, the creditor is permitted to use age as one of its factors in a credit scoring system, but if you are 62 or older you must be given at least as many points for age as any person under 62. Creditors may also consider the likelihood that the applicant's income will continue for a particular duration. An older applicant might not qualify for a large loan with a very low down payment and a shorter term. However, the creditor must apply these tests fairly and impartially.

The ECOA also requires lenders to notify the credit applicant of the decision made on their application. In the case of a credit denial, applicants must be notified of the reasons the credit was denied. The explanation must be in writing and made in within 30 days if "adverse action" is taken on a credit application. Offering different terms or a lesser amount is not considered adverse action, but rather is interpreted as a counter offer. In addition, action taken as a result of a borrower's default is not considered adverse action.

The notice required under the ECOA must contain a statement that discrimination is illegal, and include the list of factors considered discriminatory. The notice must also include the name of the federal agency responsible for enforcing the ECOA, which may vary, depending on the type of lender involved.

Credit is often denied for a combination of factors rather than for one specific factor. In the past, some creditors used a scoresheet containing certain factors, and denied credit when a certain aggregate score was not obtained. Under the ECOA, failure to attain the required score is not a sufficient reason in and of itself for denying credit. Rather, the specific reasons must be listed.

Under the Equal Credit Opportunity Act, you must be notified within 30 days after your application has been completed whether your loan has been approved or not. If credit is denied, this notice must be in writing and it must explain the specific reasons why you were denied credit or tell you of your right to ask for an explanation. You have the same rights if an account you have had is closed.

Thus, if you are denied credit, be sure to find out why. Remember, you may have to ask the creditors for this explanation. It may be that the creditor thinks you have requested more money than you can repay on your income. It may be that you have not been employed or lived long enough in the community. You can discuss terms with the creditor and ways to improve your creditworthiness.

If you think you have been discriminated against, cite the law to the lender. If the lender still denies you credit without a sufficient explanation, contact one of the consumer protection agencies for guidance and referrals.

A directory of state consumer protection agencies is set forth at Appendix 18.

If you have a complaint about a bank or other financial institution, the Federal Reserve System may be able to help you. The Federal Reserve System investigates consumer complaints received against state chartered banks that are members of the System. Complaints about these types of banks will be investigated by one of the 12 Federal Reserve Banks around the country. The Federal Reserve will refer complaints about other institutions to the appropriate federal regulatory agency and let you know where your complaint has been referred. You can contact the Federal Reserve at the following address:

Division of Consumer and Community Affairs
Board of Governors of the Federal Reserve System
Washington, D.C. 20551

HOUSING

Federal, state and local fair housing laws provide protection to prospective tenants against housing discrimination. These laws set forth the illegal reasons to refuse to rent to a tenant, and state laws may provide even greater protection. The reader is advised to check the law of his or her jurisdiction in this regard.

Landlords are still free to choose among prospective tenants, as long as their decisions comply with these laws and are based on legitimate business criteria. For example, a landlord is entitled to reject an individual who has a bad credit history, insufficient income to pay the rent, or past negative behavior—such as having caused property damage —that makes the person a bad risk. A valid occupancy policy limiting the number of people per rental, based on health and safety concerns, or on the rental property's plumbing or electrical capacities, may also be a legal basis for refusing tenants.

It is illegal for a landlord to refuse to rent to a tenant on the basis of group characteristics specified by law that are not closely related to the business needs of the landlord.

A victim of housing discrimination may file a complaint with the United States Department of Housing and Urban Development (HUD). HUD will investigate the complaint and take action if warranted. If the discrimination is a violation of a state fair housing law, the tenant may wish to file a complaint with the state agency in charge of enforcing the law. Instead of filing a complaint with HUD or a state agency, the complainant may choose to file a lawsuit directly in federal or state court.

An individual who is subjected to illegal housing discrimination is generally entitled to recover damages, which may include: (i) monetary compensation for actual damages, including reimbursement for expenses incurred in seeking alternative housing; (ii) the right to obtain the desired housing; (iii) any other damages suffered which are provable; and (iv) legal fees and costs.

Victims of housing discrimination may obtain further information and assistance by contacting HUD. In addition, many jurisdictions have their own local fair housing organizations and consumer protection agencies which can be a source of further information. Legal aid organizations may also provide free advice and/or representation to persons who qualify for services. There are also private attorneys who specialize in housing discrimination litigation.

As further discussed below, HUD enforces the federal Fair Housing Act, which prohibits discrimination based on race, color, national origin, religion, sex, family status, or disability. Nevertheless, the Federal Fair Housing Act provisions do not replace any state or local laws which provide greater requirements.

The Fair Housing Act provides that no one may take any of the following actions if based on these factors:

1. Refuse to rent or sell housing;

2. Refuse to negotiate for housing;

3. Make housing unavailable;

4. Deny a dwelling;

5. Set different terms, conditions or privileges for sale or rental of a dwelling;

6. Provide different housing services or facilities;

7. Falsely deny that housing is available for inspection, sale, or rental;

8. For profit, persuade owners to sell or rent, an activity known as blockbusting; or

9. Deny anyone access to, or membership in, a facility or service related to the sale or rental of housing.

In addition, it is illegal to (i) threaten, coerce, intimidate or interfere with anyone who is exercising a fair housing right, or assisting others who exercise that right; and to (ii) advertise or make any statement that indicates a limitation or preference based on race, color, national origin, religion, sex, familial status, or handicap.

Selected provisions of the Fair Housing Act are set forth at Appendix 19.

CHAPTER 6:
GRANDPARENT VISITATION

IN GENERAL

Family law encompasses a broad range of topics, including marriage, annulment, separation and divorce, equitable distribution, custody and visitation, and juvenile justice and children's rights. While the reader may confront one or more of these issues at some point in his or her life, of particular interest to the senior citizen is the development of the law affecting grandparent's rights.

When a senior citizen is confronted with the divorce or death of his or her own child, the senior citizen stands to lose substantial contact with not only the son or daughter-in-law, but often with his or her grandchildren of the marriage. This is a tremendously painful experience for the grandparent, which has long been overlooked and too easily dismissed by the judicial system.

A decade ago, the grandparent had little if any right to maintain contact with his or her grandchildren if the custodial parent resisted. This was particularly true when the separation was due to the death of the grandparent's own child. The other parent may go off and establish a new life with the children, in effect cutting off all communication between grandparent and child.

Although the grandparent's rights are still quite restrictive in this area, and not guaranteed, progress has been made in this direction, as further discussed below.

LEGISLATION

All 50 states have enacted statutes that provide grandparents with visitation rights as long as certain statutorily-defined criteria are met, however, no state grants an automatic right to visitation. These statutes were passed in response to legislative concerns about the effect on children of increases in divorce rates, out-of-wedlock births, teenage pregnancy, substance abuse, AIDS and child abuse and neglect. Legislatures around the country conducted extensive hearings in which citizens, physicians, psychiatrists, judges and state agencies testified to the importance of visitation between grandparents and grandchildren.

According to research compiled by the AARP, grandparents contribute significantly to the healthy development of children's emotional security and often serve as role models. Most of today's grandparents are very involved in the lives of their grandchildren. Frequently they are providers of child care. The increasing numbers of children living in single-parent families are often closer to their grandparents than children from a two-parent household. Also increasing are the numbers of grandchildren growing up in households headed by grandparents.

Factors to Be Considered

Courts are required to consider the circumstances of the individual family in deciding if a child would benefit from visits with grandparents. Some states do not permit grandparents to petition for visitation when their grandchildren's parents are married and both parents oppose visitation. Some states allow grandparents to petition for visitation even after a child is adopted by a step-parent. Some states consider an established grandparent-grandchild relationship as a factor in deciding visitation petitions.

In all 50 states, visitation is generally permitted if it meets the "best interests" of the child standard. Additional factors which may be considered include the type and duration of relationship between grandparent and grandchild and, in the case of an older child, the child's preference may be considered.

A Table of Factors Considered in Grandparent Visitation Petitions, By State, is set forth at Appendix 20.

Nevertheless, visitation is more likely to be ordered when there has been some sort of familial breakdown, e.g. divorce, separation or death. In situations where both parents are alive and still married, their wishes to alienate their children from the grandparents are likely to be honored, and some courts have deemed this to be a parent's constitutional right.

On the federal level, Congress passed Public Law 105-374 in 1998, mandating that a visitation order granted to a grandparent in one state be recognized in any state where the grandchild is living.

TROXEL V. GRANVILLE

In June 2000, the U.S. Supreme Court ruled in *Troxel v. Granville* that Washington state's visitation statute was too broadly written. In states where the statutes are more narrowly drawn, grandparents may still seek visitation. The Supreme Court decision suggests that lower courts place special weight on the opinion of parents as well as consider whether a parent has completely or unreasonably denied visitation to grandparents. As a result, it is possible that future petitions for visitation may be more closely scrutinized.

CONCLUSION

Grandparents being denied visitation with their grandchildren should know their rights under the law in the state where they are seeking visitation. In addition, if it becomes necessary to petition the court for visitation, the petitioning grandparents should seek the services of an attorney familiar with family law issues in the state where they are seeking visitation.

The lawyer referral service of state bar associations can be a useful resource for locating attorneys who specialize in this area, and legal aid offices can often be of great help to low income grandparents. Grandparents may also contact the Court Clerk's Office in their town or county for information about domestic relations or family court.

Grandparents faced with visitation issues can also obtain valuable information, support services, and referrals on a nationwide basis by contacting:

Grandparents United for Children's Rights
137 Larkin St., Madison, WI 53705
Telephone: 608-238-8751
Email: sedun@inxpress.net.

APPENDIX 1:
DIRECTORY OF NATIONAL LEGAL SERVICES FOR THE ELDERLY

NAME	ADDRESS	TELEPHONE NUMBER
American Bar Association Commission on Legal Problems of the Elderly	1800 M Street N.W., Suite 200, Washington, DC 20036	202-331-2297
Center for Social Gerentology	117 Number 1st Street, Suite 204, Ann Arbor, MI 48104	313-665-1126
Legal Counsel for the Elderly	1909 K Street N.W., Washington, DC 20049	202-434-2170
Legal Services for the Elderly	132 W. 43rd Street, 3rd Floor, New York, NY 10036	212-595-1340
Medicare Beneficiaries Defense Fund	1460 Broadway, 8th Floor, New York, NY 10036	212-869-3850
National Academy of Elder Law Attorneys	1604 N. Country Club Road, Tucson, AZ 85716	520-881-4005
National Caucus and Center on Black Aged	1424 K Street, NW, Suite 500, Washington, DC 20005	202-637-8400
National Health Law Program	2639 S. La Cienega Blvd., Los Angeles, CA 90034,	213-204-6010
National Health Law Program	2025 M Street N.W., Washington, DC 20036	202-887-5310
National Senior Citizens Law Center	1052 W. 6th Street, 7th Floor, Los Angeles, CA 90017	213-482-3550
National Senior Citizens Law Center	1101 14the Street N.W., Suite 400, Washington, DC 20005	202-887-5280

APPENDIX 2:
DIRECTORY OF STATE OFFICES OF THE AGING

STATE	NAME	ADDRESS	TELEPHONE NUMBER
Alabama	Commission on Aging	770 Washington Avenue, Suite 470 Montgomery, AL 36130	205-242-5743
Alaska	Older Alaskans Commission	Pouch C, Mail Stop 0209, Juneau, AK 99811	907-465-3250
Arizona	Aging and Adult Administration	1400 West Washington Street, Phoenix, AZ 85005	602-542-4446
Arkansas	Arkansas State Office on Aging	Donaghey Building, 7th and Main Streets Little Rock, AR 72201	501-682-2441
California	Department of Aging	1600 K Street, Sacramento, CA 95814	916-322-5290
Colorado	Aging and Adult Services Division	1575 Sherman Street, Denver, CO 80220	303-866-3851
Connecticut	Department on Aging	175 Main Street, Hartford, CT 06106	203-566-3238
Delaware	Division of Aging	1901 North Dupont Highway, New Castle, DE 19720	302-421-6791
District of Columbia	Office on Aging	1424 K Street N.W., Washington, DC 20005	202-724-5626
Florida	Program Office of Aging and Adult Services	1317 Winewood Boulevard, Tallahassee, FL 32301	904-488-8922

STATE	NAME	ADDRESS	TELEPHONE NUMBER
Georgia	Office of Aging	878 Peachtree Street N.E., Room 632 Atlanta, GA 30309	404-894-5333
Hawaii	Executive Office on Aging	1149 Bethel Street, Room 307, Honolulu, HI 96813	808-548-2593
Idaho	Office on Aging	State House, Room 108, Boise, ID 83720	208-334-3833
Illinois	Department on Aging	421 East Capitol Avenue, Springfield, IL 62706	217-785-2870
Indiana	Department on Aging & Community Services	251 N. Illinois Street, Indianapolis, IN 46204	317-232-7020
Iowa	Commission on Aging	914 Grand Avenue, Suite 236, Jewett Building, Des Moines, IA 50319	515-281-5187
Kansas	Department of Aging	915 Southwest Harrison, Topeka, KS 66612	913-296-4986
Kentucky	Division for Aging Services	275 East Main Street, 6th Floor, Frankfort, KY 40601	502-564-6930
Louisiana	Office of Elderly Affairs	4550 North Boulevard, Baton Rouge, LA 70898	504-925-1700
Maine	Bureau of Maine's Elderly	State House, Station Number 11, Augusta, ME 04333	207-626-5335
Maryland	Office on Aging	301 West Preston Street, Baltimore, MD 21201	301-225-1100
Massachusetts	Department of Elder Affairs	38 Chauncy Street, Boston, MA 02111	617-727-7750
Michigan	Office of Services to the Aging	P.O. Box 30026, Lansing, MI 48909	517-373-8230
Minnesota	Minnesota Board on Aging	444 Lafayette Road, St. Paul, MN 55155	612-296-2770

STATE	NAME	ADDRESS	TELEPHONE NUMBER
Mississippi	Mississippi Council on Aging	421 West Pascagoula Street, Jackson, MS 39203	601-354-6590
Missouri	Division on Aging	615 Howerton Court, Jefferson City, MO 65102	314-751-3082
Montana	The Governor's Office on Aging State Capitol Building	Capitol Station, Room 219, Helena, MT 59620	406-444-3111
Nebraska	Department on Aging	301 Centennial Mall South, Lincoln, NE 68509	402-471-2306
Nevada	Division of Aging Services	340 North 11th Street, Suite 114, Las Vegas, NV 89101	702-486-3545
New Hampshire	Division of Elderly and Adult Services	6 Hazen Drive, Concord, NH 03301	603-271-4680
New Jersey	Division on Aging	South Broad and Front Streets, Trenton, NJ 08625	609-292-4833
New Mexico	State Agency on Aging	224 East Palace Avenue, 4th Floor Santa Fe, NM 87501	505-827-7640
New York	Office for the Aging	Empire State Plaza, Agency Building Number 2, Albany, NY 12223	518-474-4425
North Carolina	Division of Aging	693 Palmer Drive, Suite 200, Raleigh, NC 27603	919-733-3983
North Dakota	Aging Services	State Capitol Building, Bismarck, ND 58505	701-224-2577
Ohio	Department of Aging	50 West Broad Street, 9th Floor, Columbus, OH 43215	614-466-5500
Oklahoma	Special Unit on Aging	P.O. Box 25352, Oklahoma City, OK 73125	405-521-2327
Oregon	Oregon Senior Services Division	313 Public Service Building, Salem, OR 97310	503-378-4728

STATE	NAME	ADDRESS	TELEPHONE NUMBER
Pennsylvania	Department of Aging	231 State Street, Room 307, Harrisburg, PA 17120	717-783-1550
Rhode Island	Department of Elderly Affairs	160 Pine Street, Providence, RI 02903	401-277-2858
South Carolina	Commission on Aging	400 Arbor Lake Drive, Suite B-500, Columbia, SC 29223	803-735-0210
South Dakota	Office of Adult Services and Aging	700 North Illinois Street, Pierre, SD 57501	605-773-3656
Tennessee	Commission on Aging	706 Church Street, Suite 201, Nashville, TN 37243	615-741-2056
Texas	Department on Aging	P.O. Box 12786, Capitol Station, Austin, TX 78741	512-444-2727
Utah	Division of Aging and Adult Services	120 North -200 West, Box 45500, Salt Lake City, UT 84145	801-538-3910
Vermont	Office on Aging	103 South Main Street, Waterbury, VT 05676	802-241-2400
Virginia	Office on Aging	700 East Franklin Street, Richmond, VA 23219	804-225-2271
Washington	Bureau of Aging and Adult Services Department of Social and Health Services	OB-44A Olympia, WA 98504	206-586-3768
West Virginia	Commission on Aging	State Capitol, Charleston, WV 25305	304-348-3317
Wisconsin	Bureau on Aging	217 South Hamilton Street, Suite 300 Madison, WI 53707	608-266-2536
Wyoming	Commission on Aging	Hathaway Building, Room 139, Cheyenne, WY 82002	307-777-7986

APPENDIX 3:
DIRECTORY OF NATIONAL
ORGANIZATIONS FOR THE ELDERLY

NAME	ADDRESS	TELEPHONE NUMBER
American Association of Retired Persons	1909 K Street NW, Washington, DC, 20049	202-872-4700
American Society of Aging	833 Market Street, Suite 516, San Francisco, CA 94103	415-543-2617
Choice in Dying	200 Varick Street, New York, NY 10014	212-366-5540
The Gerontological Society of America	1411 K Street NW, Suite 300, Washington, DC 20005	202-393-1411
Gray Panthers	311 S. Juniper Street, Suite 601, Philadelphia, PA 19107	215-545-6555
National Association of Area Agencies on Aging	600 Maryland Avenue SW, West Wing, Suite 208, Washington, DC 20024	202-484-7520
National Association of Retired Federal Employees	1533 New Hampshire Avenue NW, Washington, DC 20036	202-234-0832
National Association of State Units on Aging	600 Maryland Avenue SW, Suite 208, Washington, DC 20024	202-4847182
National Caucus and Center on Black Aged	1424 K Street, NW, Suite 500, Washington, DC 20005	202-637-8400
National Center on Rural Aging	600 Maryland Avenue SW, West Wing, Suite 100, Washington, DC 20024	202-479-1200

NAME	ADDRESS	TELEPHONE NUMBER
National Citizens Coalition on Nursing Home Reform	1424 16th Street NW, Suite L2, Washington, DC 20036	202-797-0657
National Council of Senior Citizens	925 15th Street, NW, Washington, DC 20005	203-347-8800
National Council on the Aging	600 Maryland Avenue SW, West Wing, Suite 100, Washington, DC 20024	202-479-1200
National Indian Council on Aging	P.O. Box 2088, Albuquerque, NM 87103	505-242-9505
National Pacific/Asian Resource Center on Aging	2033 6th Avenue, Suite 410, Seattle, WA 98121	206-448-0313
Older Women's League	666 11th Street NW, Lower Level B, Washington, DC 20005	202-783-6686
Pension Rights Center	918 16th Street NW, Suite 704, Washington, DC 20006	202-296-3776
Society for the Right to Die	250 W. 57th Street, New York, NY 10107	212-246-6973
Villers Foundation	1334 G Street NW, Washington, DC 20005	202-628-3030

APPENDIX 4:
SOCIAL SECURITY
ADMINISTRATION—REGIONAL OFFICES

REGIONAL OFFICE	AREAS COVERED
ATLANTA (REGION 1)	Alabama, Florida, Georgia, Kentucky, Mississippi, North Carolina, South Carolina, Tennessee
BOSTON (REGION 2)	Connecticut, Maine, Massachusetts, New Hampshire, Rhode Island, Vermont
CHICAGO (REGION 3)	Illinois, Indiana, Michigan, Minnesota, Ohio, Wisconsin
DALLAS (REGION 4)	Arkansas, Louisiana, Oklahoma, New Mexico, Texas
DENVER (REGION 5)	Colorado, Montana, North Dakota, South Dakota, Utah, Wyoming
KANSAS CITY (REGION 6)	Iowa, Kansas, Missouri, Nebraska
NEW YORK (REGION 7)	New York, New Jersey, Puerto Rico, Virgin Islands.
PHILADELPHIA (REGION 8)	Delaware, Maryland, Pennsylvania, Virginia, West Virginia, District of Columbia
SAN FRANCISCO (REGION 9)	Arizona, California, Hawaii, Nevada, American Samoa, Guam, Saipan
SEATTLE (REGION 10)	Alaska, Idaho, Oregon, Washington[1]

[1] Social Security Administration.

APPENDIX 5:
ELIGIBILITY AGE FOR FULL SOCIAL SECURITY BENEFITS ACCORDING TO YEAR OF BIRTH

YEAR OF BIRTH	FULL RETIREMENT AGE
1937 or earlier	65
1938	65 and 2 months
1939	65 and 4 months
1940	65 and 6 months
1941	65 and 8 months
1942	65 and 10 months
1943-1954	66
1955	66 and 2 months
1956	66 and 4 months
1957	66 and 6 months
1958	66 and 8 months
1959	66 and 10 months
1960 and later	67[1]

[1] Social Security Administration.

APPENDIX 6:
PERCENTAGE OF INCREASE IN SOCIAL SECURITY BENEFITS FOR EACH YEAR OF DELAYED RETIREMENT BEYOND FULL RETIREMENT AGE

YEAR OF BIRTH	YEARLY RATE OF INCREASE
1917-1924	3%
1925-1926	3.5%
1927-1928	4%
1929-1930	4.5%
1931-1932	5%
1933-1934	5.5%
1935-1936	6%
1937-1938	6.5%
1939-1940	7%
1941-1942	7.5%
1943 or later	8%[1]

[1] Social Security Administration.

APPENDIX 7:
SAMPLE WILL

I, Mary Jones, residing at 545 Main Street, in the Town of White Plains, Westchester County, in the State of New York, declare that this is my will. My Social Security Number is 555-55-5555.

FIRST: I revoke all wills and codicils that I have previously made.

SECOND: As used in this will, the term "specific bequest" refers to all specifically identified property that I give to one or more beneficiaries in this will. The term "residuary estate" refers to the rest of my property not otherwise specifically disposed of by this will or in any other manner. The term "residuary bequest" refers to my residuary estate that I give to one or more beneficiaries in this will.

THIRD: All personal property I give in this will through a specific or residuary bequest is given subject to any purchase-money security interest, and all real property I give in this will through a specific or residuary bequest is given subject to any deed of trust, mortgage, lien, assessment, or real property tax owed on the property. As used in this will, "purchase-money security interest" means any debt secured by collateral that was incurred for the purpose of purchasing that collateral. As used in this will, "non-purchase-money security interest" means any debt that is secured by collateral but which was not incurred for the purpose of purchasing that collateral.

FOURTH: Except for purchase money security interests on personal property passed in this will, and deeds of trust, mortgages, liens, taxes and assessments on real property passed in this will, I instruct my personal representative to pay all debts and expenses, including non-purchase-money secured debts on personal property, if any, owed by my estate as provided for by the laws of New York.

FIFTH: I instruct my personal representative to pay all estate and inheritance taxes, if any, assessed against property in my estate or against my beneficiaries as provided for by the laws of New York.

SIXTH: All the rest, residue and remainder of my estate, both real and personal, of whatsoever kind and nature and wheresoever possessed, or to which I in any way be entitled at the time of my decease, I give, devise and bequeath unto my beloved husband, JOHN JONES, if he survives me, absolutely.

SEVENTH: If my husband, JOHN JONES, shall have predeceased me, then I give, devise and bequeath my entire residuary estate, as aforesaid, unto my first alternate beneficiaries, my children, KATHLEEN JONES, born March 13, 1989; and JEANINE JONES, born November 15, 1981; and any other of my children who may be born after the date that this will is made, in equal shares. If any of my children shall have predeceased me, then I give, devise and bequeath my entire residuary estate, as aforesaid, unto my surviving children, in equal shares. I have not provided for my son, JAMES JONES, born March 27, 1973, in this will, because I have provided for him separately as a beneficiary of a life insurance policy. Notwithstanding the foregoing, if at the time of my decease, it is determined that I have no life insurance policy in effect which names my son, JAMES JONES, as beneficiary, then he is hereby named as an additional first alternate beneficiary under my will, to share equally with my other children named herein as first alternate beneficiaries.

EIGHTH: If my first alternate beneficiaries fail to survive me, I hereby give, devise and bequeath my entire residuary estate, as aforesaid, to my second alternate beneficiaries, in equal shares, as follows: To my father-in-law, CHRISTOPHER JONES, presently residing at 53 Dartmouth Street, Garden City, New York; to my father, ARTHUR SMITH, presently residing at 65-85 162nd Street, Flushing, New York; and to my mother, MARGARET SMITH, presently residing at 35-15 84th Street, Jackson Heights, New York. If any of the aforementioned second alternate beneficiaries shall have predeceased me, then I give, devise and bequeath my entire residuary estate, as aforesaid, unto the surviving second alternate beneficiaries, in equal shares.

NINTH: In the event that any of my children are minors at the time of my decease, I authorize my Personal Representative, as trustee, in his discretion, to retain the possession of the respective portion of such minors and accumulate the income therefrom during such minority, or pay over or apply the whole or any part of such principal and income to such minors, or for their support, maintenance, welfare and education, and the receipt of such payee shall be full acquittance to trustee. Any principal or income so retained or accumulated shall be paid to the minor upon attaining the age of twenty-one (21) years. Nothing herein contained shall be deemed to defer the vesting of any estate or interest in possession or otherwise.

TENTH: In the event that, upon my death, there is no living person who is entitled by law to the custody of my minor child or children, and who is available to assume such custody, I name my brother, MICHAEL SMITH, presently residing at 175 West 87th Street, Apt. 18-E, New York, New York 10024, as legal guardian of such child, to serve without bond.

ELEVENTH: When this will states that a beneficiary must survive me for the purpose of receiving a specific bequest or residuary bequest, he or she must survive me by 45 days. Notwithstanding the foregoing, property left to my spouse shall pass free of this 45-day survivorship requirement.

TWELFTH: Any specific bequest or residuary bequest made in this will to two or more beneficiaries shall be shared equally among them, unless unequal shares are specifically indicated.

THIRTEENTH: I name my husband, JOHN JONES, 545 Main Street, White Plains, New York, as my personal representative, to serve without bond. If this person shall for any reason fail to qualify or cease to act as personal representative, I name my brother, MICHAEL SMITH, 175 West 87th Street, Apt. 18-E, New York, New York 10024, as my personal representative, also to serve without bond.

FOURTEENTH: I direct my personal representative to take all actions legally permissible to have the probate of my will done as simply and as free of court supervision as possible under the laws of the state having jurisdiction over this will, including filing a petition in the appropriate court for the independent administration of my estate.

FIFTEENTH: I hereby grant to my personal representative the following powers, to be exercised as he or she deems to be in the best interests of my estate:

1. To retain property without liability for loss or depreciation resulting from such retention.

2. To dispose of property by public or private sale, or exchange, or otherwise, and receive and administer the proceeds as a part of my estate.

3. To vote stock, to exercise any option or privilege to convert bonds, notes, stocks or other securities belonging to my estate into other bonds, notes, stocks or other securities, and to exercise all other rights and privileges of a person owning similar property.

4. To lease any real property that may at any time form part of my estate.

5. To abandon, adjust, arbitrate, compromise, sue on or defend and otherwise deal with and settle claims in favor of or against my estate.

6. To continue or participate in any business which is a part of my estate, and to effect incorporation, dissolution or other change in the form of organization of the business.

7. To do all other acts which in his or her judgment may be necessary or appropriate for the proper and advantageous management, investment and distribution of my estate.

The foregoing powers, authority and discretion granted to my personal representative are intended to be in addition to the powers, authority and discretion vested in him or her by operation of law by virtue of his or her office, and may be exercised as often as is deemed necessary or advisable, without application to or approval by any court in any jurisdiction.

SIXTEENTH: If any beneficiary under this will in any manner, directly or indirectly, contests or attacks this will or any of its provisions, any share or interest in my estate given to the contesting beneficiary under this will is revoked and shall be disposed of in the same manner as if that contesting beneficiary had failed to survive me and left no living children.

SEVENTEENTH: If my spouse and I should die simultaneously, or under such circumstances as to render it difficult or impossible to determine who predeceased the other, I shall be conclusively presumed to have survived my spouse for purposes of this will.

I, Mary Jones, the testator, sign my name to this instrument, this 1st day of July, 1997. I hereby declare that I sign and execute this instrument as my last will, that I sign it willingly, and that I execute it as my free and voluntary act for the purposes therein expressed. I declare that I am of the age of majority and otherwise legally empowered to make a will, and under no constraint or undue influence. I hereby execute this will in the presence of ELEANOR JACKSON, EILEEN HARRISON and BARBARA CARTER, whom I have requested to act as witnesses.

Signature Line for Testatrix

In our presence, MARY JONES, the Testatrix, executed, published and declared that the foregoing instrument is her will, and in her presence and in the presence of each other we have signed our names below as witnesses this 1st day of July, 1997.

To the best of our knowledge, the testator is of the age of majority or otherwise legally empowered to make a will, is mentally competent, and under no constraint or undue influence.

We declare under penalty of perjury, that the foregoing is true and correct.

Signature Line for Witness #1

Address of Witness #1

Signature Line for Witness #2

Address of Witness #2

Signature Line for Witness #3

Address of Witness #3

APPENDIX 8:
STATE RULES OF INHERITANCE

STATE	APPLICABLE STATUTE	BASIC INHERITANCE RULES
Alabama	Alabama Code, Title 43, §§43-1-1 et. seq.	100% to surviving spouse if no surviving children or parents; $50,000 plus ½ of estate to surviving spouse if surviving children and all are issue of surviving spouse; ½ of estate to surviving spouse if surviving children and all not issue of surviving spouse; $100,000 plus ½ of estate to surviving spouse if surviving parents but no surviving children.
Alaska	Alaska Statutes, §13.11.005	100% to surviving spouse if no surviving children or parents; $50,000 plus ½ of estate to surviving spouse if surviving children and all issue of surviving spouse; ½ of estate to surviving spouse if surviving children and all not issue of surviving spouse; $50,000 plus ½ of estate to surviving spouse if surviving parents but no children.

STATE	APPLICABLE STATUTE	BASIC INHERITANCE RULES
Arizona	Arizona Revised Statutes, §§14-2101 et. seq.	½ of all community property to surviving spouse; 100% of community property and separate property to surviving spouse if no surviving children or if surviving children and all are issue of surviving spouse; ½ of all community property and ½ of all separate property to surviving spouse if surviving children and all not issue of surviving spouse.
Arkansas	Arkansas Statutes Annotated, §§28-8-101 et. seq.	Entire estate to surviving children or descendants of deceased children; if no such descendants then 100% to surviving spouse if married for 3 years; if not married for 3 years then 50% to surviving spouse and 50% to surviving parents; if no surviving children or spouse then 100% to surviving parents.
California	California Probate Code, §§1 et. seq.	½ of all community property and ½ of all decedent's community property to surviving spouse; 100% of all separate property to surviving spouse if no surviving children, parents, siblings or issue of siblings; ½ of separate property to surviving spouse if one surviving child, issue of deceased child, surviving parent, or issue of parent; 1/3 of separate property if more than one surviving child or issue of two or more deceased children.

STATE	APPLICABLE STATUTE	BASIC INHERITANCE RULES
Colorado	Colorado Revised Statutes, §§15-1-101 et. Seq.	100% to surviving spouse if no surviving children; $25,000 plus ½ of estate to surviving spouse if surviving children and all are issue of surviving spouse; ½ of estate to surviving spouse if surviving children and all not issue of surviving spouse.
Connecticut	Connecticut General Statutes Annotated, §§45-1 et. seq.	100% to surviving spouse if no surviving children, issue of deceased children, or surviving parents; $100,000 plus ½ of estate to surviving spouse if surviving children and all are issue of surviving spouse; ½ of estate to surviving spouse if surviving children and all not issue of surviving spouse; $100,000 plus ¾ of estate to surviving spouse if surviving parents but no surviving children; if no surviving children or spouse, 100% to surviving parents.
Delaware	Delaware Code Annotated, Title 12, §§101 et. seq.	100% to surviving spouse if no surviving children or parents; $50,000 plus ½ of personal estate and life estate in realty to surviving spouse if surviving children and all are issue of surviving spouse; ½ of personal estate and life estate in realty to surviving spouse if surviving children and all not issue of surviving spouse; $50,000 plus ½ of personal estate and life estate in realty to surviving spouse if surviving parent.

STATE	APPLICABLE STATUTE	BASIC INHERITANCE RULES
District of Columbia	District of Columbia Code, §§18-101 et. seq.	100% to surviving spouse if no surviving children, parents, grandchildren, siblings or children of siblings; 1/3 of estate to surviving spouse if surviving children or descendants of children; ½ of estate to surviving spouse if surviving parents, siblings or children of siblings, but no surviving children.
Florida	Florida Statutes Annotated, §§731.005 et. seq.	100% to surviving spouse if no surviving lineal descendants; $20,000 plus ½ of estate to surviving spouse if surviving children; ½ of estate to surviving spouse if decedent survived by a lineal descendant who is not a lineal descendant of surviving spouse.
Georgia	Georgia Statutes, Title 53, §§53-1-1 et. seq.	100% to surviving spouse if no surviving children or their descendants; child's share to surviving spouse if surviving children or their descendants; 1/5 to surviving spouse if more than five surviving children or their descendants except surviving husband always takes a child's share.
Hawaii	Hawaii Revised Statutes, §§560 et. seq.	100% to surviving spouse if no surviving children or parents; ½ of estate to surviving spouse if surviving children or parent.

STATE	APPLICABLE STATUTE	BASIC INHERITANCE RULES
Idaho	Idaho Code, §§15-1-101 et. seq.	½ of community property to surviving spouse with balance distributed to decedent's surviving descendants according to statute; 100% of separate property estate to surviving spouse if no surviving children or parents; $50,000 plus ½ of separate property estate to surviving spouse if surviving children and all are issue of surviving spouse; ½ of separate property estate to surviving spouse if surviving children and all not issue of surviving spouse; $50,000 plus ½ of separate property estate to surviving spouse if surviving parents but no surviving children.
Illinois	Illinois Annotated Statutes, Chapter 110, §§1-1 et. seq.	100% to surviving spouse if no surviving descendants; ½ of estate to surviving spouse if surviving descendants; 100% to surviving descendants if no spouse; if no surviving spouse or descendants then entire estate to surviving parents, siblings or descendants of siblings in equal share except if there is only one surviving parent he or she takes both parents share.
Indiana	Indiana Statutes Annotated, §§29-1-1 et. seq.	100% to surviving spouse if no surviving children, descendants of children, or parents; ½ of estate to surviving spouse if surviving children or descendants of children.

STATE	APPLICABLE STATUTE	BASIC INHERITANCE RULES
Iowa	Iowa Code Annotated, §§633.1 et. seq.	If no surviving children, surviving spouse receives ½ of real property, 100% of exempt personal property, and ½ of personal property after debts, but all must equal at least $50,000; if surviving children, surviving spouse receives 1/3 of real property, 100% of exempt personal property. And ½ of personal property after debts, but all must equal at least $50,000.
Kansas	Kansas Statutes Annotated, §§59-101	100% to surviving spouse if no surviving children or issue of deceased children; ½ of estate to surviving spouse if surviving children or issue of deceased children; if no surviving children, issue of deceased children or surviving spouse, 100% to surviving parents.
Kentucky	Kentucky Revised Statutes, §§391.010 et. seq.	100% to surviving spouse if no surviving children, issue of deceased children, surviving parents or siblings; ½ of personal property, fee estate in ½ of real estate and life estate in real estate to surviving spouse if surviving children, issue of deceased children, surviving parents or siblings; $7,500.00 to surviving spouse or surviving infant child.
Louisiana	Louisiana Civil Code Annotated, Article 1470 et. seq.	100% of community property if no surviving direct descendants; ½ of community property to surviving spouse if any surviving direct descendants.

STATE	APPLICABLE STATUTE	BASIC INHERITANCE RULES
Maine	Maine Revised Statutes Annotated, Title 18A, §§1-101 et. seq.	100% to surviving spouse if no surviving children or parents; $50,000 plus ½ of estate to surviving spouse if surviving children and all are issue of surviving spouse; ½ of estate to surviving spouse if surviving children and all not issue of surviving spouse; $50,000 plus ½ of estate to surviving spouse if surviving parents but no surviving children.
Maryland	Annotated Code of Maryland, Estates and Trusts Section	100% to surviving spouse if no surviving children or parents; $15,000 plus ½ of estate to surviving spouse if surviving children; ½ of estate to surviving spouse if surviving minor children; $15,000 plus ½ of estate to surviving spouse if surviving parents but no surviving children.
Massachusetts	Massachusetts General Laws Annotated, Chapter 190, §§1 et. seq.	100% to surviving spouse if no surviving children and estate does not exceed $50,000; If the estate exceeds $50,000 then $50,000 plus ½ of estate to surviving spouse; ½ of personal and real property to surviving spouse if surviving children.
Michigan	Michigan Comp. Laws Annotated, §§700.1 et. seq.	100% to surviving spouse if no surviving children or parents; $60,000 plus ½ of estate to surviving spouse if surviving children and all are issue of surviving spouse; ½ of estate to surviving spouse if surviving children and all not issue of surviving spouse; $60,000 plus ½ of estate to surviving spouse if surviving parent and no surviving children.

STATE	APPLICABLE STATUTE	BASIC INHERITANCE RULES
Minnesota	Minnesota Statutes Annotated, Chapters 524; 525 and 527	100% to surviving spouse if no surviving children; $70,000 plus ½ of estate to surviving spouse if surviving children and all are issue of surviving spouse; ½ of estate to surviving spouse if surviving children and all not issue of surviving spouse.
Mississippi	Mississippi Code Annotated, §§91-1-1 et. seq.	100% to surviving spouse if no surviving children or their descendants; if surviving children or their descendants, surviving spouse receives a child's share; children take in equal parts.
Missouri	Missouri Statutes Annotated, §§474.010 et. seq.	100% to surviving spouse if no surviving children or parents; $20,000 plus ½ of estate to surviving spouse if surviving children and all are issue of surviving spouse; ½ of estate to surviving spouse if surviving children and all not issue of surviving spouse; $20,000 plus ½ of estate to surviving spouse if surviving parents but no surviving children.
Montana	Montana Code Annotated, §§72-2-202 et. seq.	100% to surviving spouse if no surviving children or if all surviving children are issue of surviving spouse; ½ of estate to surviving spouse if one surviving child not the issue of surviving spouse; 1/3 of estate to surviving spouse if more than one surviving child not the issue of surviving spouse.

STATE	APPLICABLE STATUTE	BASIC INHERITANCE RULES
Nebraska	Revised Statutes of Nebraska, §§30-101 et. seq.	100% to surviving spouse if no surviving children or parents; $50,000 plus ½ of estate to surviving spouse if surviving children and all are issue of surviving spouse; ½ of estate to surviving spouse if surviving children and all not issue of surviving spouse; $50,000 plus ½ of estate to surviving spouse if surviving parents but no surviving children.
Nevada	Nevada Revised Statutes, Title 12, §§133.010 et. seq.	100% of community property to surviving spouse; ½ of separate property to surviving spouse if one surviving child or child's descendants; 1/3 of separate property to surviving spouse if more than one surviving child or their descendants; ½ of separate property to surviving spouse if surviving parents but no surviving children or their descendants; ½ of separate property to surviving spouse if surviving siblings but no surviving children or their descendants, or surviving parents.
New Hampshire	New Hampshire Revised Statutes Annotated, Chapter 551.1 et. seq.	100% to surviving spouse if no surviving children or parents; $50,000 plus ½ of estate to surviving spouse if surviving children and all are issue of surviving spouse; ½ of estate to surviving spouse if surviving children and all not issue of surviving spouse; $50,000 plus ½ of estate to surviving spouse if surviving parents but no surviving children.

STATE	APPLICABLE STATUTE	BASIC INHERITANCE RULES
New Jersey	Section 3B:3-1 et. Seq. of the New Jersey Statutes Annotated, §§3B: 3-1 et. seq.	100% to surviving spouse if no surviving children or parents; $50,000 plus ½ of estate to surviving spouse if surviving children and all are issue of surviving spouse; ½ of estate to surviving spouse if surviving children and all not issue of surviving spouse; $50,000 plus ½ of estate to surviving spouse if surviving parents but no surviving children.
New Mexico	New Mexico Statutes Annotated, §§45-1-101 et. seq.	100% to surviving spouse if no surviving children; 100% of community property and ¼ of separate property to surviving spouse if surviving children.
New York	Consolidated Laws of New York Annotated, EPTL §§1-1.1 et. seq.	$4,000 of personal property plus ½ of remaining personal property to surviving spouse if one surviving child or issue of deceased child; $4,000 of personal property plus 1/3 of remaining personal property to surviving spouse if more than one surviving child; $25,000 plus ½ of estate to surviving spouse if surviving parents but no surviving children.

STATE	APPLICABLE STATUTE	BASIC INHERITANCE RULES
North Carolina	General Statutes of North Carolina, §§28-A-1 et. seq.	100% to surviving spouse if no surviving children or their descendants, or surviving parents; ½ of all real property and first $15,000 of personal property plus ½ of balance of personal property to surviving spouse if one surviving child or descendant of child; 1/3 of all real property and first $15,000 of personal property plus 1/3 of balance of personal property if surviving children or descendants of children; ½ of real property and first $15,000 of personal property plus ½ of balance of personal property if surviving parents but no surviving children or descendants of children.
North Dakota	North Dakota Code, §§30.1-08-01 et. seq.	100% to surviving spouse if no surviving children or parents; $50,000 plus ½ of estate to surviving spouse if surviving children and all are issue of surviving spouse; ½ of estate to surviving spouse if surviving children and all not issue of surviving spouse; $50,000 plus ½ of estate to surviving spouse if surviving parents but no surviving children.

STATE	APPLICABLE STATUTE	BASIC INHERITANCE RULES
Ohio	Ohio Revised Code Annotated, §§2105 et. seq.	$60000 plus ½ of estate to surviving spouse if one surviving child or descendant of deceased child, if child is issue of surviving spouse; $20,000 plus ½ of estate to surviving spouse if one surviving child or descendant of deceased child, if child is not issue of surviving spouse; $60,000 plus 1/3 of estate to surviving spouse if surviving children or descendants of deceased children, and all are issue of surviving spouse; $20,000 plus 1/3 of estate to surviving spouse if surviving children or descendants of children, and all are not issue of surviving spouse.
Oklahoma	Oklahoma Statutes Annotated, Title 84, §1-308	100% to surviving spouse if no surviving children, parents or siblings; 100% of joint property plus 1/3 of balance of estate if surviving parents or siblings but no surviving children; ½ of joint property and child's share of balance of estate if surviving children or descendants of children and all not issue of surviving spouse.
Oregon	Oregon Revised Statutes, §§112.015 et. seq.	100% to surviving spouse if no surviving children; ½ of estate to surviving spouse if surviving children.
Pennsylvania	Pennsylvania Statutes Annotated, Title 20, §§101 et. seq.	100% to surviving spouse if no surviving children or parents; $30,000 plus ½ of estate to surviving spouse if surviving children and all are issue of surviving spouse; ½ of estate to surviving spouse if surviving children and all not issue of surviving spouse; $30,000 plus ½ of estate to surviving spouse if surviving parents but no surviving children.

STATE	APPLICABLE STATUTE	BASIC INHERITANCE RULES
Rhode Island	General Laws of Rhode Island, §§33-1-1 et. seq.	All real property to surviving spouse for life subject to any encumbrances; 100% of entire estate to surviving spouse if no surviving children or kindred; $50,000 plus ½ of personal property to surviving spouse if surviving kindred but no surviving children; ½ of personal property to surviving spouse if surviving children.
South Carolina	Code of Laws of South Carolina, §§21-1-10 et. seq.	100% to surviving spouse if no surviving children or their descendants parents, or siblings; ½ of estate to surviving spouse if one surviving child; 1/3 of estate to surviving spouse if more than one surviving child.
South Dakota	South Dakota Comp. Laws Annotated, §§29-1-1 et. seq.	½ of estate to surviving spouse if one surviving child or descendant of deceased child; 1/3 of estate to surviving spouse if more than one surviving child, or one surviving child and surviving descendants of deceased children; 100% of estate to surviving children or descendants of deceased children if no surviving spouse; $100,000 plus ½ of balance of estate to surviving spouse if surviving parents, siblings or descendants of siblings, but no surviving children.
Tennessee	Tennessee Code Annotated, §§30-101 et. seq.	100% to surviving spouse if no surviving children or their descendants; child's share not less than 1/3 of estate to surviving spouse if surviving children or their descendants.

STATE	APPLICABLE STATUTE	BASIC INHERITANCE RULES
Texas	Texas Probate Code, §§1 et. seq.	100% of community property to surviving spouse if no surviving children or their descendants; ½ of community property to surviving spouse if surviving children or their descendants; 100% of personal property and ½ of real property to surviving spouse if no surviving children or their descendants with balance to decedent's other surviving relatives; 1/3 of personal property and a life estate in 1/3 of real property to surviving spouse if surviving children or their descendants.
Utah	Utah Code, §§75-1-101 et. seq.	100% to surviving spouse if no surviving children or parents; $50,000 plus ½ of estate to surviving spouse if surviving children and all are issue of surviving spouse; ½ of estate to surviving spouse if surviving children and all not issue of surviving spouse; $100,000 plus ½ of estate to surviving spouse if surviving parents but no surviving children.
Vermont	Vermont Statutes Annotated, Title 14, §§1 et. seq.	Surviving spouse takes dower or curtesy equal to 1/3 of real property; If no surviving children, surviving spouse inherits $25,000 plus ½ of remainder; if decedent leaves no surviving kindred, surviving spouse inherits the entire estate; if decedent leaves surviving children, surviving spouse's share limited to dower or curtesy.

STATE	APPLICABLE STATUTE	BASIC INHERITANCE RULES
Virginia	Code of Virginia, §§64.1 et. seq.	All personal and real property in fee simple to surviving spouse unless decedent survived by children or their descendants who are not children of surviving spouse in which case 1/3 of personal and real property to surviving spouse and 2/3 to decedent's surviving children and their descendants.
Washington	Revised Code of Washington Annotated, §§11.02.005 et. seq.	100% of community property to surviving spouse; ½ of separate property to surviving spouse if surviving children; ¾ of separate property to surviving spouse if surviving parents or siblings; 100% of separate property to surviving spouse if no surviving children, parents or siblings.
West Virginia	West Virginia Code, §§41-1-1 et. seq.	Dower interest of 1/3 of all real property as life estate to surviving spouse; 1/3 of all personal property to surviving spouse if surviving children or their descendants; 100% of all personal property and real property to surviving spouse if no surviving children or their descendants.

STATE	APPLICABLE STATUTE	BASIC INHERITANCE RULES
Wisconsin	Wisconsin Statutes Annotated, §§852.01 et. seq.	100% of estate to surviving spouse if no surviving children; first $25,000 plus ½ of balance of estate to surviving spouse if one surviving child of the marriage, or children of a deceased child of the marriage; first $25,000 plus 1/3 of balance of estate to surviving spouse if more than one surviving child of the marriage, or children of deceased child of the marriage; ½ of the estate to surviving spouse if surviving children not of the marriage, or children of a deceased child not of the marriage.
Wyoming	Wyoming Statutes Annotated, §§2-1-101 et. seq.	100% to surviving spouse if no surviving children or their descendants; ½ of estate to surviving spouse if surviving children and their descendants; ½ of estate to surviving spouse if surviving parents or siblings, but no surviving children or their descendants.

APPENDIX 9:
STATE LAW EXCEPTIONS TO
CONVENTIONAL PROBATE

STATE	APPLICABLE STATUTE	PROBATE EXEMPTION	SIMPLIFIED PROBATE
Alabama	Alabama Code, Title 43, Chapter 2, §§690, et. seq.	Not Available	Yes—up to $3,000 of personal property
Alaska	Alaska Statutes, Title 13, Chapter 6, § 13.16.08	Not Available	Yes—no dollar limit
Arizona	Arizona Revised Statutes, §§14-3971, et. seq.	Yes—up to $30,000 of personal property	Not available except for certain types of family property
Arkansas	Arkansas Statutes Annotate, §§G2.2127, et. seq.	Yes—up to $25,000	Not Available
California	California Probate Code, §§13200, et. seq.	Yes—up to $60,000 of personal property and real property interest	$10,000, No dollar limit to surviving spouse on community property petition
Colorado	Colorado Revised Statutes, §§15-12-1201	Yes—up to $20,000 of net estate	Not available except for certain types of family property
Connecticut	Connecticut General Statutes Annotated, Title 45, §§266 et. seq.	Not Available	Yes—Up to $10,000 to spouse, next of kin, or creditor

STATE	APPLICABLE STATUTE	PROBATE EXEMPTION	SIMPLIFIED PROBATE
Delaware	Delaware Code Annotated, Title 12, §2306 et. seq.	Yes—up to $12,500 of personal property to spouse, grandparents, children or other statutory relative	Not Available
District of Columbia	District of Columbia Code, Title 20, §§2101 et. seq.	Not Available	Yes—up to $10,000 of personal property
Florida	Florida Statutes Annotated, §§735.103 et. Seq.; 735.201 et. Seq.; and 735.301 et. seq.	Not Available	Yes—Up to $25,000 of Florida property and up to $60,000 of estate to family members
Georgia	None	Not Available	Not Available
Hawaii	Hawaii Revised Statutes, §§560:3-1205 et. Seq.; and 560:3-1213	Yes—up to $2,000	Yes—up to $20,000 of Hawaii property
Idaho	Idaho Code, §15-3-301, et. seq.	Not Available	Yes—no dollar limit
Illinois	Illinois Annotated Statutes, Chapter 110-1/2, §§6-8, et. Seq.; 9-8, et. Seq.; and 25-1, et. seq.	Yes—up to $25,000 of personal property; or if all beneficiaries are Illinois residents and are in agreement and no state of federal estate taxes are due	Yes—up to $50,000
Indiana	Indiana Statutes Annotated, §§27-1-7.5-5, et. Seq.; and 29-1-8-2, et. seq.	Yes—up to $8,500 of personal property	Yes—no dollar limit

STATE	APPLICABLE STATUTE	PROBATE EXEMPTION	SIMPLIFIED PROBATE
Iowa	Iowa Code Annotated, §635, et. seq.	Not Available	Yes—up to $15,000 of total value of Iowa property to surviving spouse, minor children or parents only
Kansas	Kansas Statutes Annotated, §§59-3201, et. Seq.; and 59-3301, et. seq.	Not Available	Yes—no dollar limit
Kentucky	Kentucky Revised Statutes, §§391.030, et. Seq. and 395.450, et. seq	Not Available	Yes—by agreement of all beneficiaries or when estate to spouse is under $7,500
Louisiana	No applicable statute	Not Available	Only if resident dies intestate with estate under $50,000
Maine	Maine Revised Statutes Annotated, Title 18A, §1-101	Not Available	Yes—no dollar limit
Maryland	Annotated Code of Maryland, §§5-601, et. seq.	Not available	Yes—up to $20,000
Massachusetts	Massachusetts General Laws Annotated, Chapter 195, §§16, et. seq.	Not Available	Yes—up to $15,000 of personal property
Michigan	Michigan Comp. Laws Annotated, §§9.1936; 27.5101, et. Seq.; and 257.236	Not available	Yes—up to $5,000
Minnesota	Minnesota Statutes Annotated, §§525.51, et. seq.	Not Available	Yes—up to $30,000

STATE	APPLICABLE STATUTE	PROBATE EXEMPTION	SIMPLIFIED PROBATE
Mississippi	Mississippi Code Annotated, §91-7-147	Not Available	Yes—up to $500
Missouri	Missouri Statutes Annotated, §5-473.097	Not Available	Yes—up to $15,000
Montana	Montana Code Annotated, Title 72, §§3-201, et. seq.	Not Available	Yes—up to $15,000
Nebraska	Revised Statutes of Nebraska, §§30-2414, et. seq.	Not Available	Yes—no dollar limit
Nevada	Nevada Revised Statutes, §§145.070, et. Seq. And 146.010, et. seq.	Yes—up to $25,000	Yes—up to $100,000
New Hampshire	New Hampshire Revised Statutes Annotated, Chapter 553,331, et. seq.	Not Available except up to $500 to surviving spouse	Yes—up to $5,000
New Jersey	No applicable statute	Not available except $10,000 to spouse and $5,000 to others if resident dies intestate	Not Available
New Mexico	New Mexico Statutes, §§45-3-1202 and 45-3-1204	Yes—up to $5,000	Yes—up to $10,000
New York	Consolidated Laws of New York Annotated, EPTL §§1301, et. seq.	Yes—up to $10,000 and certain exempt property	Not Available
North Carolina	General Statutes of North Carolina, Chapter 28A, §25-1.1	Yes—up to $10,000 personal property	Not Available

STATE	APPLICABLE STATUTE	PROBATE EXEMPTION	SIMPLIFIED PROBATE
North Dakota	North Dakota Code, §§30.1-14, et. seq.	Not Available	Yes—no dollar limit
Ohio	Ohio Revised Code Annotated, §2113.02	Not Available	Yes—up to $15,000
Oklahoma	Oklahoma Statutes Annotated, Title 58, §§241, et. seq.	Not Available	Yes—up to $60,000
Oregon	Oregon Revised Statutes, §§114.515, et. seq.	Yes—up to $15,000 personal property and $35,000 real property	Not Available
Pennsylvania	Pennsylvania Statutes Annotated, Title 20, §§3102, et. seq.	Not Available	Yes—up to $10,000 personal property
Rhode Island	No applicable statute	Not Available	Not Available
South Carolina	Code of Laws of South Carolina, Title 62, Chapter 3, §§1201 and 1203, et. seq.	Yes—up to $10,000	Yes—up to $10,000
South Dakota	South Dakota Codified Laws, §§30-11A, et. Seq.; and 30-11-1	Yes—up to $5,000	Yes—up to $60,000
Tennessee	Tennessee Code Annotated, Title 30, Chapter 4, §§101, et. seq.	Not Available	Yes—up to $10,000 real property
Texas	Texas Probate Code, §§137, et. Seq. And 145, et. seq.	Yes—up to $50,000	Yes—no dollar limit
Utah	Utah Code, Title 75, §3-301	Not Available	Yes—no dollar limit

STATE	APPLICABLE STATUTE	PROBATE EXEMPTION	SIMPLIFIED PROBATE
Vermont	Vermont Statutes Annotated, Title 14, §§1901, et. seq.	Not Available	Yes—up to $10,000 personal property
Virginia	Code of Virginia, §§64.1-132, et. seq.	Yes—up to $5,000 personal property and $5,000 wages or bank account	Not Available
Washington	Revised Code of Washington Annotated, Title 11, §§62.010, et. seq.	Yes—up to $10,000 personal property	Not Available
West Virginia	West Virginia Code, Chapter 24, Article 2, §1	Not Available	Yes—up to $50,000
Wisconsin	Wisconsin Statutes Annotated, §§867.03, et. Seq. And 867.045, et. seq.	Yes—up to $5,000 personal property	Yes—up to $10,000
Wyoming	Wyoming Statutes Annotated, §2-1-201	Yes—up to $30,000	Not Available

APPENDIX 10:
SAMPLE CODICIL TO A WILL

On July 1, 1997, I, MARY JONES, executed my will in the presence of the following witnesses:

1. Eleanor Jackson

2. Eileen Harrison

3. Barbara Carter

I hereby make this first codicil to my will, as follows:

Whereas in paragraph designated ELEVENTH of my will I appointed my husband, JOHN JONES, as my executor, I now wish to name my father, ARTHUR SMITH, to act as my executor, also to serve without bond.

I hereby execute this codicil on January 1, 19__, in the presence of Eleanor Jackson, Eileen Harrison and Barbara Carter, whom I requested to act as witnesses.

Signature Line for Testatrix

In our presence, MARY JONES, the Testatrix, executed, published and declared that the foregoing instrument is the first codicil to his will, and in his presence and in the presence of each other we have signed our names below as witnesses this 1st day of January, 19__.

Signature Line for Witness #1

Signature Line for Witness #2

Signature Line for Witness #3

APPENDIX 11:
MEDICARE PATIENTS' STATEMENT OF RIGHTS

As a Medicare beneficiary, you have certain guaranteed rights. These rights protect you when you get health care; they assure you access to needed health care services; and they protect you against unethical practices. You have these Medicare rights whether you are in the Original Medicare Plan or another Medicare health plan. Your rights include:

1. The right to protection from discrimination in marketing and enrollment practices.

2. The right to information about what is covered and how much you have to pay.

3. The right to information about all treatment options available to you. You have the right to information about all your health care treatment options from your health care provider. Medicare forbids its health plans from making any rules that would stop a doctor from telling you everything you need to know about your health care, including treatment options. If you think your Medicare health plan may have kept your health care provider from telling you everything you need to know about your health care treatment options, you have a right to appeal.

4. The right to receive emergency care. If you have severe pain, an injury, sudden illness, or a suddenly worsening illness that you believe may cause your health serious danger without immediate care, you have the right to receive emergency care. You never need prior approval for emergency care, and you may receive emergency care anywhere in the United States.

5. The right to appeal decisions to deny or limit payment for medical care. If you are in the Original Medicare Plan, you have the right to appeal a denial of payment for a service you have been provided. Likewise, if you are enrolled in one of the other Medicare health plans, you have the right to appeal the plan's denial for a service to

be provided. As a Medicare beneficiary, you always have the right to appeal these decisions.

6. The right to know how your Medicare health plan pays its doctors. If you request information on how a Medicare health plan pays its doctors, the plan must give it to you in writing. You also have the right to know whether your doctor has a financial interest in a health care facility, such as a laboratory, since it could affect the medical advice he or she gives you.

7. The right to choose a women's health specialist.

8. The right, if you have a complex or serious medical condition, to receive a treatment plan that includes direct access to a specialist.

If you believe that any of your rights have been violated, please call the State Health Insurance Assistance Program in your State.[1]

---

1   Source: Social Security Administration.

APPENDIX 12:
THE PRESCRIPTION DRUG FAIRNESS FOR SENIORS ACT (H.R. 664)

A BILL

To provide for substantial reductions in the price of prescription drugs for Medicare beneficiaries.

Be it enacted by the Senate and House of Representatives of the United States of America in Congress assembled,

SECTION 1. SHORT TITLE.

This Act may be cited as the 'Prescription Drug Fairness for Seniors Act of 1999'.

SEC. 2. FINDINGS AND PURPOSES.

(a) FINDINGS—The Congress finds the following:

(1) Manufacturers of prescription drugs engage in price discrimination practices that compel many older Americans to pay substantially more for prescription drugs than the drug manufacturers' most favored customers, such as health insurers, health maintenance organizations, and the Federal Government.

(2) On average, older Americans who buy their own prescription drugs pay twice as much for prescription drugs as the drug manufacturers' most favored customers. In some cases, older Americans pay over 15 times more for prescription drugs than the most favored customers.

(3) The discriminatory pricing by major drug manufacturers sustains their annual profits of $20,000,000,000, but causes financial hardship and impairs the health and well-being of millions of older Americans. More than one in eight older Americans are forced to choose between buying their food and buying their medicines.

(4) Most federally funded health care programs, including Medicaid, the Veterans Health Administration, the Public Health Service, and the Indian Health Service, obtain prescription drugs for their beneficiaries at low prices. Medicare beneficiaries are denied this benefit and cannot obtain their prescription drugs at the favorable prices available to other federally funded health care programs.

(5) Implementation of the policy set forth in this Act is estimated to reduce prescription drug prices for Medicare beneficiaries by more than 40 percent.

(6) In addition to substantially lowering the costs of prescription drugs for older Americans, implementation of the policy set forth in this Act will significantly improve the health and well-being of older Americans and lower the costs to the Federal taxpayer of the Medicare program.

(7) Older Americans who are terminally ill and receiving hospice care services represent some of the most vulnerable individuals in our nation. Making prescription drugs available to Medicare beneficiaries under the care of Medicare-certified hospices will assist in extending the benefits of lower prescription drug prices to those most vulnerable and in need.

(b) PURPOSE—The purpose of this Act is to protect Medicare beneficiaries from discriminatory pricing by drug manufacturers and to make prescription drugs available to Medicare beneficiaries at substantially reduced prices.

SEC. 3. PARTICIPATING MANUFACTURERS.

(a) IN GENERAL—Each participating manufacturer of a covered outpatient drug shall make available for purchase by each pharmacy such covered outpatient drug in the amount described in subsection (b) at the price described in subsection (c).

(b) DESCRIPTION OF AMOUNT OF DRUGS—The amount of a covered outpatient drug that a participating manufacturer shall make available for purchase by a pharmacy is an amount equal to the aggregate amount of the covered outpatient drug sold or distributed by the pharmacy to Medicare beneficiaries.

(c) DESCRIPTION OF PRICE—The price at which a participating manufacturer shall make a covered outpatient drug available for purchase by a pharmacy is the price equal to the lower of the following:

(1) The lowest price paid for the covered outpatient drug by any agency or department of the United States.

(2) The manufacturer's best price for the covered outpatient drug, as defined in section 1927(c)(1)(C) of the Social Security Act (42 U.S.C. 1396r-8(c)(1)(C)).

SEC. 4. SPECIAL PROVISION WITH RESPECT TO HOSPICE PROGRAMS.

For purposes of determining the amount of a covered outpatient drug that a participating manufacturer shall make available for purchase by a pharmacy under section 3, there shall be included in the calculation of such amount the amount of the covered outpatient drug sold or distributed by a pharmacy to a hospice program. In calculating such amount, only amounts of the covered outpatient drug furnished to a Medicare beneficiary enrolled in the hospice program shall be included.

SEC. 5. ADMINISTRATION.

The Secretary shall issue such regulations as may be necessary to implement this Act.

SEC. 6. REPORTS TO CONGRESS REGARDING EFFECTIVENESS OF ACT.

(a) IN GENERAL—Not later than 2 years after the date of the enactment of this Act, and annually thereafter, the Secretary shall report to the Congress regarding the effectiveness of this Act in—

(1) protecting Medicare beneficiaries from discriminatory pricing by drug manufacturers, and

(2) making prescription drugs available to Medicare beneficiaries at substantially reduced prices.

(b) CONSULTATION—In preparing such reports, the Secretary shall consult with public health experts, affected industries, organizations representing consumers and older Americans, and other interested persons.

(c) RECOMMENDATIONS—The Secretary shall include in such reports any recommendations they consider appropriate for changes in this Act to further reduce the cost of covered outpatient drugs to Medicare beneficiaries.

SEC. 7. DEFINITIONS.

In this Act:

(1) PARTICIPATING MANUFACTURER—The term 'participating manufacturer' means any manufacturer of drugs or biologicals that, on

or after the date of the enactment of this Act, enters into a contract or agreement with the United States for the sale or distribution of covered outpatient drugs to the United States.

(2) COVERED OUTPATIENT DRUG—The term 'covered outpatient drug' has the meaning given that term in section 1927(k)(2) of the Social Security Act (42 U.S.C. 1396r-8(k)(2)).

(3) MEDICARE BENEFICIARY—The term 'Medicare beneficiary' means an individual entitled to benefits under part A of title XVIII of the Social Security Act or enrolled under part B of such title, or both.

(4) HOSPICE PROGRAM—The term 'hospice program' has the meaning given that term under section 1861(dd)(2) of the Social Security Act (42 U.S.C. 1395x(dd)(2)).

(5) SECRETARY—The term 'Secretary' means the Secretary of Health and Human Services.

SEC. 8. EFFECTIVE DATE.

The Secretary shall implement this Act as expeditiously as practicable and in a manner consistent with the obligations of the United States.

APPENDIX 13:
DIRECTORY OF STATE OFFICES OF
LONG-TERM CARE OMBUDSMAN

STATE	NAME	ADDRESS	TELEPHONE NUMBER
Alabama	Commission on Aging	136 Catoma Street, 2nd Floor, Montgomery, AL 36130	205-242-5743
Alaska	Office of the Older Alaskans Ombudsman	3601 C Street, Suite 260, Anchorage, AK 99503	907-279-2232
Arizona	Aging and Adult Administration	1400 West Washington Street, Phoenix, AZ 85005	602-542-4446
Arkansas	Arkansas State Office on Aging	1417 Donaghey Plaza South, Little Rock, AR 72203	501-682-8952
California	Department of Aging	1600 K Street, Sacramento, CA 95814	916-322-6681
Colorado	Aging and Adult Services Division	455 Sherman Street, Denver, CO 80203	303-722-0300
Connecticut	Department on Aging	175 Main Street, Hartford, CT 06106	203-566-7770

STATE	NAME	ADDRESS	TELEPHONE NUMBER
Delaware	Division of Aging	1113 Church Avenue, Milford, DE 19963	302-422-1386
District of Columbia	Office on Aging	1909 K Street N.W., Washington, DC 20049	202-833-6720
Florida	Program Office of Aging and Adult Services	154 Holland Avenue, Tallahassee, FL 32399	904-488-6190
Georgia	Office of Aging	878 Peachtree Street N.E., Room 632, Atlanta, GA 30309	404-894-5336
Hawaii	Executive Office on Aging	335 Merchant Street, Room 241, Honolulu, HI 96813	808-548-2539
Idaho	Office on Aging	State House, Room 114, Boise, ID 83720	208-334-3833
Illinois	Department on Aging	421 East Capitol Avenue, Springfield, IL 62706	217-785-3140
Indiana	Department on Aging & Community Services	251 N. Illinois Street, Indianapolis, IN 46204	317-232-7020
Iowa	Commission on Aging	914 Grand Avenue, Suite 236, Jewett Building, Des Moines, IA 50319	515-281-5187
Kansas	Department of Aging	915 Southwest Harrison, Topeka, KS 66612	913-296-4986
Kentucky	Division for Aging Services	275 East Main Street, 6th Floor, Frankfort, KY 40601	502-564-6930

STATE	NAME	ADDRESS	TELEPHONE NUMBER
Louisiana	Office of Elderly Affairs	4528 Bennington Avenue, LA 70898	504-925-1700
Maine	Commission on Aging	State House, Station number 127, Augusta, ME 04333	207-289-3658
Maryland	Office on Aging	301 West Preston Street, Baltimore, MD 21201	301-225-1083
Massachusetts	Department of Elder Affairs	38 Chauncy Street, Boston, MA 02111	617-727-7273
Michigan	Citizens for Better Care	1627 East Kalamazoo, Lansing, MI 48912	517-482-1297
Minnesota	Office of Ombudsman for Older Minnesotans	444 Lafayette Road, St. Paul, MN 55155	612-296-3969
Mississippi	Mississippi Council on Aging	421 West Pascagoula Street, Jackson, MS 39203	601-949-2070
Missouri	Division on Aging	2701 West Main Street, Jefferson City, MO 65102	314-751-3082
Montana	Seniors' Office of Legal and Ombudsman Services	P.O. Box 232, Capitol Station, Helena, MT 59620	406-444-4676
Nebraska	Department on Aging	301 Centennial Mall South, Lincoln, NE 68509	402-471-2306
Nevada	Division of Aging Services	340 North 11th Street, Suite 114, Las Vegas, NV 89101	702-486-3545

STATE	NAME	ADDRESS	TELEPHONE NUMBER
New Hampshire	Division of Elderly and Adult Services	6 Hazen Drive, Concord, NH 03301	603-271-4375
New Jersey	Office of the Ombudsman for the Institutionalized Elderly	28 West State Street, Room 305, Trenton, NJ 08625	609-292-8016
New Mexico	State Agency on Aging	224 East Palace Avenue, 4th Floor, Santa Fe, NM 87501	505-827-7640
New York	Office for the Aging	Empire State Plaza, Agency Building Number 2, Albany, NY 12223	518-474-7329
North Carolina	Division of Aging	693 Palmer Drive, Raleigh, NC 27603	919-733-8400
North Dakota	Aging Services	State Capitol Building, Bismarck, ND 58505	701-224-2577
Ohio	Department of Aging	50 West Broad Street, 9th Floor, Columbus, OH 43215	614-466-9927
Oklahoma	Special Unit on Aging	P.O. Box 25352, Oklahoma City, OK 73125	405-521-6734
Oregon	Office of Long-Term Care Ombudsman	2475 Lancaster Drive, Building B, Number 9, Salem, OR 97310	503-378-6533
Pennsylvania	Department of Aging	231 State Street, Harrisburg, PA 17120	717-783-7247
Rhode Island	Department of Elderly Affairs	160 Pine Street, Providence, RI 02903	401-277-6883

STATE	NAME	ADDRESS	TELEPHONE NUMBER
South Carolina	Division of Ombudsman and Citizens' Service	1205 Pendleton Street, Columbia, SC 29201	803-734-0457
South Dakota	Office of Adult Services and Aging	700 North Illinois Street, Pierre, SD 57501	605-773-3656
Tennessee	Commission on Aging	706 Church Street, Suite 201, Nashville, TN 37243	615-741-2056
Texas	Department on Aging	P.O. Box 12786, Capitol Station, Austin, TX 78741	512-444-2727
Utah	Division of Aging and Adult Services	120 North - 200 West, Box 45500, Salt Lake City, UT 84145	801-538-3924
Vermont	Office on Aging	103 South Main Street, Waterbury, VT 05676	802-241-2400
Virginia	Office on Aging	700 East Frannklin Street, Richmond, VA 23219	804-225-2271
Washington	South King County Multi-Service Center	1200 S. 336 Street, Federal Way, Olympia, WA 98003	206-838-6810
West Virginia	Commission on Aging	State Capitol, Charleston, WV 25305	304-558-3317
Wisconsin	Board on Aging and Long Term Care	214 North Hamilton Street, Madison, WI 53703	608-266-8944
Wyoming	State Bar Association	900 8th Street, Wheatland, WY 82201	307-322-5553

APPENDIX 14:
SAMPLE LIVING WILL

DECLARATION made this (enter date).

I, (Name and address), being of sound mind, willfully and voluntarily make known my desire that my life shall not be artificially prolonged under the circumstances set forth below, and do hereby declare:

MEDICAL CONDITION

1. If at any time I should have a terminal or incurable condition caused by injury, disease, or illness, certified to be terminal or incurable by at least two physicians, which within reasonable medical judgment would cause my death, and where the application of life-sustaining procedures would serve only to artificially prolong the moment of my death, I direct that such procedures be withheld or withdrawn, and that I be permitted to die with dignity.

2. If at any time I experience irreversible brain injury, or a disease, illness, or condition that results in my being in a permanent, irreversible vegetative or comatose state, and such injury, disease, illness, or condition would preclude any cognitive, meaningful, or functional future existence, I direct my physicians and any other attending nursing or health care personnel to allow me to die with dignity, even if that requires the withdrawal or withholding of nutrition or hydration and my death will follow such withdrawal or withholding.

LIFE-SUSTAINING PROCEDURES

It is my expressed intent that the term "life-sustaining procedures" shall include not only medical or surgical procedures or interventions that utilize mechanical or other artificial means to sustain, restore, or supplant a vital function, but also shall include the placement, withdrawal, withholding, or maintenance of nasogastric tubes, gastrostomy, intravenous lines, or any other artificial, surgical, or invasive means for nutritional support and/or hydration.

"Life-sustaining procedures" shall not be interpreted to include the administration of medication or the performance of any medical procedure deemed necessary to provide routine care and comfort or alleviate pain.

RIGHT TO REFUSE TREATMENT

It is my intent and expressed desire that this Declaration shall be honored by my family, physicians, nurses, and any other attending health care personnel as the final expression of my constitutional and legal right to refuse medical or surgical treatment and to accept the consequences of such refusal. Any ambiguities, questions, or uncertainties that might arise in the reading, interpretation, or implementation of this Declaration shall be resolved in a manner to give complete expression to my legal right to refuse treatment and shall be construed as clear and convincing evidence of my intentions and desires.

REVOCATION OF PREVIOUSLY EXECUTED DOCUMENTS

I understand the full importance of this Declaration and I am emotionally and mentally competent to make this Declaration, and by my execution, I hereby revoke any previously executed Health Care Declaration.

COPIES AND DISTRIBUTION

The original of this document is kept at (address where kept). I have made (#) copies of this document. Numbered and signed copies have been provided to the following individuals or institutions: (List names, addresses and phone numbers of individuals and institutions).

STATEMENT OF WITNESSES

I state this (enter date), under penalty of perjury, that the Declarant has identified (himself or herself) to me and that the Declarant signed or acknowledged this Health Care Declaration in my presence.

I believe the Declarant to be of sound mind, and the Declarant has affirmed (his or her) awareness of the nature of this document and is signing it voluntarily and free from duress. The Declarant requested that I serve as a witness to (his or her) execution of this document.

I declare that I am not related to the Declarant by blood, marriage, or adoption and that to the best of my knowledge I am not entitled to any part of the estate of the Declarant on the death of the principal under a will or by operation of law.

I am not a provider of health or residential care, an employee of a provider of health or residential care, the operator of a community care facility, or an employee of an operator of a health care facility.

I declare that I have no claim against any portion of the estate of the Declarant upon (his or her) death, nor any personal financial responsibility for the payment of Declarant's medical bills or any other of Declarant's obligations.

Signature Line of Witness #1

Address of Witness #1

Signature Line of Witness #2

Address of Witness #2

Signature Line of Witness #3

Address of Witness #3

Subscribed and acknowledged before me by the Declarant, (Name), and by his or her witnesses (Names) on (enter date).

Notary Signature and Stamp

APPENDIX 15:
TABLE OF STATE LIVING WILL STATUTES

STATE	STATUTE	SECTION
Alabama	Natural Death Act	Code of Alabama §22-8A-1 et seq.
Alaska	Rights of Terminally Ill Act	Alaska Statutes §18.12.010 et seq.
Arizona	Medical Treatment Decision Act	Arizona Revised Statutes §36-3261
Arkansas	Rights of the Terminally Ill or Permanently Unconscious Act	Arkansas Statutes Annotated §20-17-201 et seq.
California	Natural Death Act	California Health & Safety Code §7188
Colorado	Medical Treatment Decision Act	Colorado Revised Statutes §15-18-101
Connecticut	Removal of Life Support Systems	Connecticut General Statutes Annotated §19a-570 et seq.
Delaware	Delaware Death with Dignity Act	Delaware Code Annotated Title 16 §2501 et seq.
District of Columbia	Natural Death Act	District of Columbia Code Title 6 §2421 et seq.
Florida	Life Prolonging Procedure Act	Florida Statutes Annotated §765.101 et seq.
Georgia	Living Wills Act	Code of Georgia §31-32-1
Hawaii	Medical Treatment Decisions Act	Hawaii Revised Statutes §327D

STATE	STATUTE	SECTION
Idaho	Natural Death Act	Idaho Code §39-4501 et seq.
Illinois	Living Will Act	Illinois Revised Statutes Chapter 110-1/2 §701 et seq.
Indiana	Living Wills and Life Prolonging Procedures Act	Indiana Code Annotated §16-8-11-1 et seq.
Iowa	Life Sustaining Procedures Act	Code of Iowa §144A.
Kansas	Natural Death Act	Kansas Statutes Annotated §65-28103(a) e. seq.
Kentucky	Living Will Act	Kentucky Revised Statutes §311.624 et seq.
Louisiana	Natural Death Act	Louisiana Revised Statutes §40:1299.58.
Maine	Living Will Act	Maine Revised Statutes Annotated Title 18-A §5-701 et seq.
Maryland	Life Sustaining Procedures Act	Maryland Health General Code Annotated §5-601 et seq.
Massachusetts	No statutory provision	
Michigan	No statutory provision	
Minnesota	Adult Health Care Decisions Act	Minnesota Statutes §145B.03 et seq.
Mississippi	Natural Death Act	Mississippi Code Annotated41-41-105 et seq.
Missouri	Life Support Declaration	Annotated Missouri Statutes §459.010 et seq.
Montana	Living Will Act	Revised Montana Code Annotated §50-9-101 et seq.
Nebraska	No statutory provision	
Nevada	Living Will Statute	Nevada Revised Statutes §449.600

STATE	STATUTE	SECTION
New Hampshire	Terminal Care Document	New Hampshire Revised Statutes Annotated 137-H §§1-16
New Jersey	Living Will Statute	New Jersey Statutes Annotated Chapter 201
New Mexico	Right to Die Act	New Mexico Statutes Annotated §24-7-1 et seq.
New York	No statutory provision	
North Carolina	Natural Death Act	General Statutes of North Carolina §90-320 et seq.
North Dakota	Uniform Rights of Terminally Ill Act	North Dakota Century Code §23-06.4
Ohio	Living Will Statute	Ohio Revised Code Annotated §2133.01 et seq.
Oklahoma	Natural Death Act	Oklahoma Statutes Annotated §663-3101.1 et seq.
Oregon	Directive to Physicians	Oregon Revised Statutes §127.610 et seq.
Pennsylvania	No statutory provision	
Rhode Island	No statutory provision	
South Carolina	Death with Dignity Act	Code of Laws of South Carolina §44-77-10 et seq.
South Dakota	Living Will Statute	South Dakota Codified Laws Annotated §34-12D
Tennessee	Right to Natural Death Act	Tennessee Code Annotated §32-11-101 et seq.
Texas	Natural Death Act	Texas Revised Civil Statutes Annotated §672.004 et seq.
Utah	Personal Choice and Living Will Act	Utah Code Annotated §75-2-1101 et seq.
Vermont	Terminal Care Document	Vermont Statutes Annotated Title 18 §5251
Virginia	Natural Death Act	Code of Virginia Annotated §54.1-2981 et seq.

STATE	STATUTE	SECTION
Washington	Natural Death Act	Washington Revised Code Annotated §70-122.010 et seq.
West Virginia	Natural Death Act	West Virginia Code Chapter 16 Article 30 et seq.
Wisconsin	Natural Death Act	Wisconsin Statutes Annotated §154.01 et seq.
Wyoming	Living Will Act	Wyoming Statutes 35-22-102 et seq.

APPENDIX 16:
SAMPLE DURABLE POWER OF ATTORNEY
FOR HEALTH CARE

APPOINTMENT made this (enter date).

I, (Name and address), being of sound mind, willfully and voluntarily appoint (name, address, city, state, phone), as my Health Care Agent (hereinafter "Agent") with a Durable Power of Attorney to make any and all health care decisions for me, except to the extent stated otherwise in this document.

EFFECTIVE DATE

This Durable Power of Attorney and Appointment of Health Care Agent shall take effect at such time as I become comatose, incapacitated, or otherwise mentally or physically incapable of giving directions or consent regarding the use of life-sustaining procedures or any other health care measures.

"Health care" in this context means any treatment, service, or procedure utilized to maintain, diagnose, or treat any physical or mental condition.

DETERMINATION OF MEDICAL CONDITION

A determination of incapacity shall be certified by my attending physician and by a second physician who is neither employed by the facility where I am a patient nor associated in practice with my attending physician and who shall be appointed to independently assess and evaluate my capacity by the appropriate administrator of the facility where I am a patient.

AUTHORITY OF HEALTH CARE AGENT

My Agent is authorized, in consultation with my attending physician, to direct the withdrawal or withholding of any life-sustaining procedures, as defined herein, as (he or she) solely in the exercise of (his or her) judgment shall determine are appropriate to give comply with my wishes and desires.

In addition, my Agent by acceptance of this Appointment agrees and is hereby directed to use (his or her) best efforts to make those decisions that I would make in the exercise of my right to refuse treatment and not those that (he or she) or others might believe to be in my best interests.

APPOINTMENT OF ALTERNATE AGENTS

If the person designated as my Agent is unable or unwilling to accept this Appointment, I designate the following persons to serve as my Agent to make health care decisions for me as authorized by this document. They shall serve in the following order:

1. First Alternate Agent: (name, address and telephone)

2. Second Alternate Agent: (name, address and telephone)

DURATION

I understand that this Power of Attorney exists indefinitely unless I define a shorter time herein or execute a revocation. If I am incapacitated at such time as this Power of Attorney expires (if applicable), the authority I have granted my Agent shall continue until such time as I am capable of giving directions regarding my health care.

(If applicable:) This power of attorney ends on the following date:

COPIES AND DISTRIBUTION

The original of this document is kept at (address where kept). I have made (#) copies of this document. Numbered and signed copies have been provided to the following individuals or institutions: (List names, addresses and phone numbers of individuals and institutions).

STATEMENT OF WITNESSES

I state this (enter date), under penalty of perjury, that the Declarant has identified (himself or herself) to me and that the Declarant signed or acknowledged this Durable Power of Attorney and Appointment of Health Care Agent in my presence.

I believe the Declarant to be of sound mind, and the Declarant has affirmed (his or her) awareness of the nature of this document and is signing it voluntarily and free from duress. The Declarant requested that I serve as a witness to (his or her) execution of this document.

I am not the person appointed as Agent by this document, and I am not a provider of health or residential care, an employee of a provider of health or residential care, the operator of a community care facility, or an employee of an operator of a health care facility.

I declare that I am not related to the Declarant by blood, marriage, or adoption and that to the best of my knowledge I am not entitled to any part of the estate of the Declarant on the death of the principal under a will or by operation of law.

I declare that I have no claim against any portion of the estate of the Declarant upon (his or her) death, nor any personal financial responsibility for the payment of Declarant's medical bills or any other of Declarant's obligations.

Signature Line of Witness #1

Address of Witness #1

Signature Line of Witness #2

Address of Witness #2

Signature Line of Witness #3

Address of Witness #3

Subscribed and acknowledged before me by the Declarant, (Name), and by his or her witnesses (Names) on (enter date).

Notary Signature and Stamp

APPENDIX 17:
NATIONAL DIRECTORY OF ORGANIZATIONS SUPPORTING CHOICE FOR TERMINALLY ILL PATIENTS

NAME	ADDRESS	TELEPHONE
Americans for Death with Dignity	1783 Terrace Drive, Belmont, CA 94002	415-593-28631
Center for Social Gerentology	117 number 1st Street, Suite 204, Ann Arbor, MI 48104	313-665-1126
Choice in Dying	475 Riverside Drive, Room 1852, New York, NY 10115	212-870-2003
Compassion in Dying	6312 S.W. Capitol Highway, Suite 415, Portland, OR 97201	503-221-9556
Death with Dignity Education Center	520 El Camino Real, Suite 710, San Mateo, CA 94402-1720	415-344-6489
Dying Well Network	P.O. Box 880, Spokane, WA 99210	509-926-2457
Euthanasia Research & Guidance Organization (ERGO)	24829 Norris Lane, Junction City, Oregon 97448-9559	541-998-1873
Hemlock Society USA	P.O. Box 101810, Denver, CO 80250	303-639-1202
Life-Fax, IDR Technology Inc.	P.O. Box 501136, Atlanta, GA 31150	404-696-0377
Legal Counsel for the Elderly	1909 K Street N.W., Washington, DC 20049	202-434-2170

NAME	ADDRESS	TELEPHONE
Legal Services for the Elderly	132 W. 43rd Street, 3rd Floor, New York, NY 10036	212-595-1340
Merian's Friends	P.O. Box 272, Northville, MI 48167	888-217-0700
National Health Law Program	2639 S. La Cienega Blvd., Los Angeles, CA 90034	213-204-6010
National Health Law Program	2025 M Street N.W., Washington, DC 20036	202-887-5310
National Senior Citizens Law Center	1052 W. 6th Street, 7th Floor, Los Angeles, CA 90017	213-482-3550
National Senior Citizens Law Center	2025 M Street N.W, Suite 400, Washington, DC 20036	202-887-5280

APPENDIX 18:
DIRECTORY OF STATE CONSUMER
PROTECTION AGENCIES

STATE	ADDRESS	TELEPHONE NUMBER
Alabama	Consumer Protection Division, Office of the Attorney General, 11 S. Union Street, Montgomery, AL 36130	205-261-7334
Alaska	Consumer Protection Section, Office of the Attorney General, 1031 W. 4th Avenue, Suite 110-B, Anchorage, AK 99501	907-279-0428
Arizona	Financial Fraud Division, Office of the Attorney General, 1275 W. Washington St., Phoenix, AZ 85007	602-542-3702
Arkansas	Consumer Protection Division, Office of the Attorney General, 200 Tower Building, 4th & Center Streets, Little Rock, AR 72201	501-682-2007
California	Public Inquiry Unit, Office of the Attorney General, 1515 K Street., Suite 511, Sacramento, CA 94244-2550	916-322-3360
California	Consumer Protection Division, Los Angeles City Attorney's Office, 200 N. Main Street, 1600 City Hall East, Los Angeles, CA 90012	213-485-4515
Colorado	Consumer Protection Unit, Office of the Attorney General, 1525 Sherman Street, 3rd Floor, Denver, CO 80203	303-866-5167
Connecticut	Department of Consumer Protection, 165 Capitol Avenue, Hartford, CT 06106	203-566-4999

STATE	ADDRESS	TELEPHONE NUMBER
Delaware	Division of Consumer Affairs, Department of Community Affairs, 820 N. French Street, 4th Floor, Wilmington, DE 19801	302-571-3250
District of Columbia	Department of Consumer & Regulatory Affairs, 614 H Street NW, Washington, DC 20001	202-737-7000
Florida	Division of Consumer Services, 218 Mayo Building, Tallahassee, FL 32399	904-488-2226
Georgia	Governor's Office of Consumer Affairs, 2 Martin Luther King Jr. Drive SE Plaza Level, E Tower, Atlanta, GA 30334	404-656-7000
Hawaii	Office of Consumer Protection, 828 Fort St. Mall, Honolulu, HI 96812-3767	808-548-2560
Idaho	None Listed	
Illinois	Consumer Protection Division, Office of the Attorney General, 100 W. Randolph Street, 12th Floor, Chicago, IL 60601	312-917-3580
Indiana	Consumer Protection Division, Office of the Attorney General, 219 State House, Indianapolis, IN 46204	317-232-6330
Iowa	Consumer Protection Division, Office of the Attorney General, 1300 E. Walnut Street, 2nd Floor, Des Moines, IA 50319	515-281-5926
Kansas	Consumer Protection Division, Office of the Attorney General, Kansas Judicial Center, 2nd Floor, Topeka, KS 66612	913-296-3761
Kentucky	Consumer Protection Division, Office of the Attorney General, 209 St. Clair Street, Frankfort, KY 40601	502-564-2200
Louisiana	Consumer Protection Section, Office of the Attorney General, State Capitol Building, P.O. Box 94005, Baton Rouge, LA 70804	504-342-7013

STATE	ADDRESS	TELEPHONE NUMBER
Maine	Consumer and Antitrust Division, Office of the Attorney General, State House Station #6, Augusta, ME 04333	207-289-3716
Maryland	Consumer Protection Division, Office of the Attorney General, 7 N. Calvert Street, 3rd Floor, Baltimore, MD 21202	301-528-8662
Massachusetts	Consumer Protection Division, Office of the Attorney General, One Ashburton Place, Room 1411, Boston, MA 02108	617-727-7780
Michigan	Consumer Protection Division, Office of the Attorney General, 670 Law Building, Lansing, MI 48913	517-373-1140
Minnesota	Office of Consumer Services, Office of the Attorney General, 117 University Avenue, St. Paul, MN 55155	612-296-2331
Mississippi	Consumer Protection Division, Office of the Attorney General, P.O. Box 220,, Jackson, MS 39205	601-359-3680
Missouri	Trade Offense Division, Office of the Attorney General, P.O. Box 899, Jefferson City, MO 65102	314-751-2616
Montana	Consumer Affairs Unit, Department of Commerce, 1424 9th Avenue, Helena, MT 59620	406-444-4312
Nebraska	Consumer Protection Division, Department of Justice, 2115 State Capitol, P.O. Box 98920, Lincoln, NE 68509	402-471-4723
Nevada	Department of Commerce, State Mail Room Complex, Las Vegas, NV 89158	702-486-4150
New Hampshire	Consumer Protection and , Antitrust Division, Office of the Attorney General, State House Annex, Concord, NH 03301	603-271-3641
New Jersey	Division of Consumer Affairs, 1100 Raymond Boulevard, Room 504, Newark, NJ 07102	201-648-4010

STATE	ADDRESS	TELEPHONE NUMBER
New Mexico	Consumer and Economic Crime Division, Office of the Attorney General, P.O. Box Drawer 1508, Santa Fe, NM 87504	505-872-6910
New York	Consumer Protection Board, 99 Washington Avenue, Albany, NY 12210	518-474-8583
New York	Consumer Protection Board, 250 Broadway,17th Floor, New York, NY 10007-2593	212-587-4908
North Carolina	Consumer Protection Section, Office of the Attorney General, P.O. Box 629, Raleigh, NC 27602	919-733-7741
North Dakota	Consumer Fraud Division, Office of the Attorney General, State Capitol Building, Bismarck, ND 58505	701-224-2210
Ohio	Consumer Frauds and Crimes Section, Office of the Attorney General, 30 E. Broad Street, 25th Floor, Columbus, OH 43266-0410	614-466-4986
Oklahoma	Consumer Affairs, Office of the Attorney General, 112 State Capitol Building, Oklahoma City, OK 73105	405-521-3921
Oregon	Financial Fraud Section, Office of the Attorney General, Justice Building, Salem, OR 97310	503-378-4320
Pennsylvania	Bureau of Consumer Protection, Office of the Attorney General, Strawberry Square, 14th Floor, Harrisburg, PA 17120	717-787-9707
Rhode Island	Consumer Protection Division, Office of the Attorney General, 72 Pine Street, Providence, RI 02903	401-277-2104
South Carolina	Department of Consumer Affairs, P.O. Box 5757, Columbia, SC 29250	803-734-9452
South Dakota	Division of Consumer Affairs, Office of the Attorney General, State Capitol Building, Pierre, SD 57501	605-773-4400

STATE	ADDRESS	TELEPHONE NUMBER
Tennessee	Division of Consumer Affairs, Department of Commerce & Insurance500 James Robertson Parkway, 5th Floor, Nashville,TN 37219	615-741-4737
Texas	Consumer Protection Division, Office of the Attorney General, Box 12548, Capitol Station, Austin,TX 78711	512-463-2070
Utah	Division of Consumer Protection, Department of Business Regulation, 160 E. Third South, P.O. Box 45802, Salt Lake City,UT 84145	801-530-6601
Vermont	Public Protection Division, Office of the Attorney General, 109 State Street, Montpelier, VT 05602	802-828-3171
Virginia	Division of Consumer Counsel, Office of the Attorney General, Supreme Court Building, 101 N. 8th Street, Richmond, VA 23219	804-786-2116
Washington	Consumer and Business Fair Practices Division, 710 2nd Avenue, Suite 1300, Seattle,WA 98104	206-464-7744
West Virginia	Consumer Protection Division, Office of the Attorney General, 812 Quarrier Street, 6th Floor, Charleston, WV 25301	304-348-8986
Wisconsin	Office of Consumer Protection, Department of Justice, P.O. Box 7856, Madison,WI 53707	608-266-1852
Wyoming	Office of the Attorney General, 123 State Capitol Building, Cheyenne,WY 82002	307-777-6286

Source: Consumers Resource Handbook, U.S. Office of Consumer Affairs, 1990.

APPENDIX 19:
DIRECTORY OF HUD FAIR HOUSING OFFICES

AREAS COVERED	NAME	ADDRESS	LOCAL TELEPHONE	TOLL-FREE TELEPHONE	TTY
Connecticut, Maine, Massachusetts, New Hampshire, Rhode Island and Vermont	U.S. Department of Housing and Urban Development	Thomas P. O'Neill, Jr. Federal Building, 10 Causeway Street, Room 321, Boston, Massachusetts 02222-1092	(617) 565-5308	1-800-827-5005	(617) 565-5453
New Jersey and New York	U.S. Department of Housing and Urban Development	26 Federal Plaza, Room 3532, New York, New York 10278-0068	(212) 264-9610	1-800-496-4294	(212) 264-0927

AREAS COVERED	NAME	ADDRESS	LOCAL TELEPHONE	TOLL-FREE TELEPHONE	TTY
Delaware, District of Columbia, Maryland, Pennsylvania, Virginia and West Virginia	U.S. Department of Housing and Urban Development	The Wanamaker Building, 100 Penn Square East, Philadelphia, Pennsylvania 19107-3380	(215) 656-0660	1-888-799-2085	(215) 656-3450
Alabama, the Caribbean, Florida, Georgia, Kentucky, Mississippi, North Carolina, South Carolina and Tennessee	U.S. Department of Housing and Urban Development	Richard B. Russell Federal Building, 75 Spring Street SW, Room 230, Atlanta, Georgia 30303-3388	(404) 331-5140	1-800-440-8091	(404) 730-2654
Illinois, Indiana, Michigan, Minnesota, Ohio and Wisconsin	U.S. Department of Housing and Urban Development	Ralph H. Metcalfe Federal Building, 77 West Jackson Boulevard, Room 2101, Chicago, Illinois 60604-3507	(312) 353-7776	1-800-765-9372	(312) 353-7143
Arkansas, Louisiana, New Mexico, Oklahoma and Texas	U.S. Department of Housing and Urban Development	1600 Throckmorton, Room 502, Fort Worth, Texas 76113-2905	(817) 978-9270	1-800-498-9371	(817) 978-9274

AREAS COVERED	NAME	ADDRESS	LOCAL TELEPHONE	TOLL-FREE TELEPHONE	TTY
Iowa, Kansas, Missouri and Nebraska	U.S. Department of Housing and Urban Development	Gateway Tower II, 400 State Avenue, Room 200, Kansas City, Kansas 66101-2406	(913) 551-6958	1-800-743-5323	(913) 551-6972
Colorado, Montana, North Dakota, South Dakota, Utah and Wyoming	U.S. Department of Housing and Urban Development	633 17th Street, Denver, Colorado 80202-3607	(303) 672-5437	1-800-877-7353	(303) 672-5248
Arizona, California, Hawaii and Nevada	U.S. Department of Housing and Urban Development	Phillip Burton Federal Building and U.S. Courthouse, 450 Golden Gate Avenue, San Francisco, California 94102-3448	(415) 436-840	1-800-347-3739	(415) 436-6594
Alaska, Idaho, Oregon and Washington	U.S. Department of Housing and Urban Development	Seattle Federal Office Building, 909 First Avenue, Room 205, Seattle, Washington 98104-1000	(206) 220-5170	1-800-877-0246	(206) 220-5185

APPENDIX 20:
TABLE OF FACTORS TO BE CONSIDERED IN EVALUATING GRANDPARENT VISITATION PETITION BY STATE

STATE	FACTORS TO BE CONSIDERED
Alabama	Best Interests of Child, Effect on Parent/Child Relationship
Alaska	Best Interests of Child, Prior Grandparent/Grandchild Relationship
Arizona	Best Interests of Child, Prior Grandparent/Grandchild Relationship
Arkansas	Best Interests of Child
California	Best Interests of Child, Prior Grandparent/Grandchild Relationship, Effect on Parent/Child Relationship
Colorado	Best Interests of Child
Connecticut	Best Interests of Child
Delaware	Best Interests of Child
Florida	Best Interests of Child, Prior Grandparent/Grandchild Relationship, Effect on Parent/Child Relationship
Georgia	Best Interests of Child, Must Show Harm
Hawaii	Best Interests of Child
Idaho	Best Interests of Child
Illinois	Best Interests of Child
Indiana	Best Interests of Child, Prior Grandparent/Grandchild Relationship
Iowa	Best Interests of Child, Prior Grandparent/Grandchild Relationship

STATE	FACTORS TO BE CONSIDERED
Kansas	Best Interests of Child, Prior Grandparent/Grandchild Relationship
Kentucky	Best Interests of Child
Louisiana	Best Interests of Child
Maine	Best Interests of Child, Prior Grandparent/Grandchild Relationship, Effect on Parent/Child Relationship
Maryland	Best Interests of Child
Massachusetts	Best Interests of Child
Michigan	Best Interests of Child
Minnesota	Best Interests of Child, Prior Grandparent/Grandchild Relationship, Effect on Parent/Child Relationship
Mississippi	Best Interests of Child, Prior Grandparent/Grandchild Relationship
Missouri	Best Interests of Child
Montana	Best Interests of Child
Nebraska	Best Interests of Child, Prior Grandparent/Grandchild Relationship, Effect on Parent/Child Relationship
Nevada	Best Interests of Child, Prior Grandparent/Grandchild Relationship, Effect on Parent/Child Relationship
New Hampshire	Best Interests of Child, Prior Grandparent/Grandchild Relationship, Effect on Parent/Child Relationship
New Jersey	Best Interests of Child, Prior Grandparent/Grandchild Relationship, Effect on Parent/Child Relationship
New Mexico	Best Interests of Child, Prior Grandparent/Grandchild Relationship
New York	Best Interests of Child
North Carolina	Best Interests of Child, Prior Grandparent/Grandchild Relationship
North Dakota	Best Interests of Child, Prior Grandparent/Grandchild Relationship
Ohio	Best Interests of Child
Oklahoma,	Best Interests of Child, Prior Grandparent/Grandchild Relationship, Effect on Parent/Child Relationship
Oregon	Best Interests of Child, Prior Grandparent/Grandchild Relationship

STATE	FACTORS TO BE CONSIDERED
Pennsylvania	Best Interests of Child, Prior Grandparent/Grandchild Relationship, Effect on Parent/Child Relationship
Rhode Island	Best Interests of Child,
South Carolina	Best Interests of Child, Prior Grandparent/Grandchild Relationship, Effect on Parent/Child Relationship
South Dakota	Best Interests of Child, Illinois Street, Pierre, SD 57501, 605-773-3656
Tennessee	Best Interests of Child, Prior Grandparent/Grandchild Relationship, Effect on Parent/Child Relationship
Texas	Best Interests of Child, Prior Grandparent/Grandchild Relationship
Utah	Best Interests of Child
Vermont	Best Interests of Child, Prior Grandparent/Grandchild Relationship, Effect on Parent/Child Relationship
Virginia	Best Interests of Child, Effect on Parent/Child Relationship
Washington,	Best Interests of Child, Prior Grandparent/Grandchild Relationship, Effect on Parent/Child Relationship
West Virginia	Best Interests of Child, Prior Grandparent/Grandchild Relationship, Effect on Parent/Child Relationship
Wisconsin	Best Interests of Child, Prior Grandparent/Grandchild Relationship
Wyoming	Best Interests of Child, Effect on Parent/Child Relationship

Source: American Association of Retired Persons.

GLOSSARY

Acknowledgement—A formal declaration of one's signature before a notary public.

Active Euthanasia—The inducement of gentle death solely by means without which life would continue naturally.

Actuary—One who computes various insurance and property costs, and calculates the cost of life insurance risks and insurance premiums.

Adhesion Contract—An adhesion contract is a standardized contract form offered to consumers of goods and services on a "take it or leave it" basis without affording the consumer a realistic opportunity to bargain, and under such conditions that infer coercion.

Administrator—The person appointed by the court to settle the estate of a deceased person if he or she dies intestate.

Affidavit—A sworn or affirmed statement made in writing and signed; if sworn, it is notarized.

American Bar Association (ABA)—A national organization of lawyers and law students.

American Civil Liberties Union (ACLU)—A nationwide organization dedicated to the enforcement and preservation of rights and civil liberties guaranteed by the federal and state constitutions.

Annuity—The right to receive fixed, periodic payments over a specified term.

Asset—The entirety of a person's property, either real or personal.

Assignee—An assignee is a person to whom an assignment is made, also known as a grantee.

Assignment—An assignment is the transfer of an interest in a right or property from one party to another.

Attending Physician—The doctor who is the primary caregiver for a particular patient.

Attestation—The act of witnessing an instrument in writing at the request of the party making the same, and subscribing it as a witness.

Attorney In Fact—An attorney-in-fact is an agent or representative of another given authority to act in that person's name and place pursuant to a document called a "power of attorney."

Beneficiary—A person who is designated to receive property upon the death of another, such as the beneficiary of a life insurance policy, who receives the proceeds upon the death of the insured.

Bequest—Refers to a gift of personal property contained in a will.

Bill of Rights—The first eight amendments to the United States Constitution.

Capacity—Capacity is the legal qualification concerning the ability of one to understand the nature and effects of one's acts.

Chattel—Article of personal property.

Child Custody—The care, control and maintenance of a child which may be awarded by a court to one of the parents of the child.

Civil Rights Act of 1964—The federal act passed to provide stronger protection for rights guaranteed by the Constitution, such as voting rights.

Codicil—A document modifying an existing will which, in order to be valid, must be formally drafted and witnessed according to statutory requirements.

Collateral—Property which is pledged as additional security for a debt, such as a loan.

Community Property—A form of ownership in a minority of states where a husband and wife are deemed to own property in common, including earnings, each owning an undivided one-half interest in the property.

Confidence Game—A scheme where the perpetrator wins the confidence of his or her victim in order to cheat the victim out of a sum of money or other valuable.

Consanguinity—Related by blood.

Consecutive—In criminal law, refers to sentences which are to be served in numerical order.

Conservator—A conservator is the court-appointed custodian of property belonging to a person determined to be unable to properly manage his or her property.

Consortium—The conjugal association of husband and wife, and the right of each to the company and care of the other.

Constitution—The fundamental principles of law which frame a governmental system.

Constitutional Right—Refers to the individual liberties granted by the constitution of a state or the federal government.

Consumer Credit—Loans and sale credit extended to individuals to finance the purchases of goods and services arising out of consumer needs and desires.

Coroner—The public official whose responsibility it is to investigate the circumstances and causes of deaths which occur within his or her jurisdiction.

Credit—Credit is that which is extended to the buyer or borrower on the seller or lender's belief that that which is given will be repaid.

Credit Report—A credit report refers to the document from a credit reporting agency setting forth a credit rating and pertinent financial data concerning a person or a company, which is used in evaluating the applicant's financial stability.

Decedent—A deceased person.

Decree—A decision or order of the court.

Deductible—An amount an insured person must pay before they are entitled to recover money from the insurer, in connection with a loss or expense covered by an insurance policy.

Deed—A legal instrument conveying title to real property.

Dividends—A payment which a corporation makes to its shareholders according to the number of shares outstanding.

Domicile—The one place designated as an individual's permanent home.

Due Process Rights—All rights which are of such fundamental importance as to require compliance with due process standards of fairness and justice.

Durable Power of Attorney—Also known as a "health care proxy," refers to a document naming a person to make a medical decisions in the event that the individual becomes unable to make those decisions himself or herself.

Duress—Refers to the action of one person which compels another to do something he or she would not otherwise do.

Duty—The obligation, to which the law will give recognition and effect, to conform to a particular standard of conduct toward another.

Earned Income—Income which is gained through one's labor and services, as opposed to investment income.

Elective Share—Statutory provision that a surviving spouse may choose between taking that which is provided in the spouse's will, or taking a statutorily prescribed share.

Employee Retirement Income Security Act of 1974 (ERISA)—A federal statute which governs the administration of pension plans.

Equitable Distribution—The power of the courts to equitably distribute all property legally and beneficially acquired during marriage by either spouse, whether legal title lies in their joint or individual names.

Escheat—The reversion of private property to the government under certain conditions, e.g. the absence of an heir.

Escrow—The arrangement for holding instruments or money which is not to be released until certain specified conditions are met.

Estate—The entirety of one's property, real or personal.

Estate Tax—A tax levied on a decedent's estate in connection with the right to transfer property after death.

Euthanasia—The act of painlessly assisting in the death of persons suffering from terminal illness or other prolonged suffering. Literally means "good death" in Greek.

Execution—The performance of all acts necessary to render a written instrument complete, such as signing, sealing, acknowledging, and delivering the instrument; also refers to supplementary proceedings to enforce a judgment, which, if monetary, involves a direction to the sheriff to take the necessary steps to collect the judgment.

Executor—A person appointed by the maker of a will to carry out his or her wishes concerning the administration and distribution of his or estate according to the terms of a will.

Executor's Deed—A deed given by an executor or other fiduciary which conveys real property.

Exemption—A tax deduction granted a taxpayer who has a certain status, e.g. aged 65 or over.

Face Value—The value of an insurance policy upon the death of the insured.

Fee Simple Absolute—A real property estate giving the owner the most absolute power over the title available.

FHA Mortgage—A mortgage insured by the Federal Housing Administration.

Fiduciary—A fiduciary is a person having a legal duty, created by an undertaking, to act primarily for the benefit of another in matters connected with the undertaking.

Finance Charge—Any charge for an extension of credit, such as interest.

Fixed Income—Income which is unchangeable.

Fraud—A false representation of a matter of fact, whether by words or by conduct, by false or misleading allegations, or by concealment of that which should have been disclosed, which deceives and is intended to deceive another, and thereby causes injury to that person.

Fraudulent Conveyance—The transfer of property for the purpose of delaying or defrauding creditors.

Gift Tax—A tax assessed against the transferor of a gift of property, based upon the fair market value of the property on the date transferred.

Grace Period—In contract law, a period specified in a contract which is beyond the due date but during which time payment will be accepted without penalty.

Grantee—One who receives a conveyance of real property by deed.

Grantor—One who conveys real property by deed.

Guardian—A person who is entrusted with the management of the property and/or person of another who is incapable, due to age or incapacity, to administer their own affairs.

Guardian Ad Litem—Person appointed by a court to represent a minor or incompetent for purpose of some litigation

Heir—One who inherits property.

Heirs—Those individuals who, by law, inherit an estate of an ancestor who dies without a will.

Hereditament—Anything which can be inherited.

Hereditary Succession—The passing of title to an estate according to the laws of descent.

Illegal—Against the law.

Incapacity—Incapacity is a defense to breach of contract which refers to a lack of legal, physical or intellectual power to enter into a contract.

Incompetency—Lack of legal qualification or fitness to discharge a legally required duty or to handle one's own affairs; also refers to matters not admissible in evidence.

Indigent—A person who is financially destitute.

Individual Retirement Account (IRA)—A retirement plan for individuals who are not eligible for pension or profit-sharing plans.

Informed Consent—The requirement that a patient be apprised of the nature and risks of a medical procedure before the physician can validly claim exemption from liability for battery, or from responsibility for medical complications.

Inherit—To take as an heir at law by descent rather than by will.

Inheritance—Property inherited by heirs according to the laws of descent and distribution.

Inheritance Tax—A tax levied on heirs in connection with the right to receive property from a decedent's estate.

Insurance—A contingency agreement, supported by consideration, whereby the insured receives a benefit, e.g. money, in the event the contingency occurs.

Inter Vivos—Latin for "between the living." Refers to transactions made during the lifetime of the parties.

Interest—An amount of money paid by a borrower to a lender for the use of the lender's money.

Interest Rate—The percentage of a sum of money charged for its use.

Intestate—The state of dying without having executed a valid will.

Intestate Succession—The manner of disposing of property according to the laws of descent and distribution when the decedent died without leaving a valid will.

Irrevocable Trust—A trust that cannot be canceled by the person who established it.

Joint Tenancy—The ownership of property by two or more persons who each have an undivided interest in the whole property, with the right of survivorship, whereby upon the death of one joint tenant, the remaining joint tenants assume ownership.

Judgment Creditor—A creditor who has obtained a judgment against a debtor, which judgment may be enforced to obtain payment of the amount due.

Judgment Debtor—An individual who owes a sum of money, and against whom a judgment has been awarded for that debt.

Judgment Proof—Refers to the status of an individual who does not have the financial resources or assets necessary to satisfy a judgment.

Legacy—A gift of personal property by will.

Legal Aid—A national organization established to provide legal services to those who are unable to afford private representation.

Legal Capacity—Referring to the legal capacity to sue, it is the requirement that a person bringing the lawsuit have a sound mind, be of lawful age, and be under no restraint or legal disability.

Legatee—One who takes a legacy.

Letters of Administration—A formal document issued by a court which authorizes a person to act as an administrator for the estate of a deceased person.

Life Estate—An estate in land held during the term of a specified person's life.

Life Expectancy—The period of time which a person is statistically expected to live, based on such factors as their present age and sex.

Life Insurance—A contract between an insured and an insurer whereby the insurer promises to pay a sum of money upon the death of the insured to his or her designated beneficiary, in return for the periodic payment of money, known as a premium.

Living Trust—A trust which is operated during the life of the creator of the trust.

Living Will—A declaration that states an individual's wishes concerning the use of extraordinary life support systems.

Long Term Care—The services provided at home or in an institutionalized setting to older persons who require medical or personal care for an extended period of time.

Maintenance—The furnishing by one person to another the means of living, or food, clothing, shelter, etc., particularly where the legal relations of the parties is such that one is bound to support the other, as between parent and child or between spouses

Maker—As used in commercial law, the individual who executes a note.

Marital Property—Property purchased by persons while married to each other.

Maturity Date—The date upon which a creditor is designated to receive payment of a debt, such as payment of the principal value of a bond to a bondholder by the issuing company or governmental entity.

Medical Malpractice—The failure of a physician to exercise that degree of skill and learning commonly applied under all the circumstances in the community by the average prudent reputable professional in the same field.

Medicare—The program governed by the Social Security Administration to provide medical and hospital coverage to the aged or disabled.

Mortgage—A written instrument, duly executed and delivered, that creates a lien upon real estate as security for the payment of a specific debt.

Narcotics—Generic term for any drug which dulls the senses or induces sleep and which commonly becomes addictive after prolonged use.

Net Estate—The gross estate less the decedent's debts, funeral expenses and any other deductions proscribed by law.

Net Income—Gross income less deductions and exemptions proscribed by law.

Net Worth—The difference between one's assets and liabilities.

Nonfreehold Estate—A leasehold.

Note—A writing which promises payment of a debt.

Notice of Petition—Written notice of a petitioner that a hearing will be held in a court to determine the relief requested in an annexed petition.

Oath—A sworn declaration of the truth under penalty of perjury.

Obligee—An obligee is one who is entitled to receive a sum of money or performance from the obligor.

Obligor—An obligor is one who promises to perform or pay a sum of money under a contract.

Ombudsman—Under certain state laws, an individual licensed to oversee various health care issues.

Parens Patriae—Latin for "parent of his country." Refers to the role of the state as guardian of legally disabled individuals.

Party—Person having a direct interest in a legal matter, transaction or proceeding.

Pension Plan—A retirement plan established by an employer for the payment of pension benefits to employees upon retirement.

Petition—A formal written request to a court which initiates a special proceeding.

Petitioner—In a special proceeding, one who commences a formal written application, requesting some action or relief, addressed to a court for determination.

Portfolio—The entirety of one's financial investments.

Post Mortem—Latin for "after death." Refers to the coroner's examination of a body to determine cause of death.

Power of Attorney—A legal document authorizing another to act on one's behalf.

Premium—The periodic payment of money by an insured to an insurer for insurance protection against specified losses.

Probate—The process of proving the validity of a will and administering the estate of a decedent.

Promissory Note—A written promise by the maker to pay a certain sum of money to the payee or his order on demand or on a fixed date.

Real Estate—The land and all the things permanently attached to it.

Real Property—Land, and generally whatever is erected or growing upon or affixed to the land.

Redlining—An illegal form of discrimination whereby a lender denies credit based on the characteristics of the borrower's neighborhood.

Residuary Clause—The clause in a will which conveys to the residuary beneficiaries any property of the testator which was not specifically given to a particular legatee.

Statute—A law.

Succession—The process by which a decedent's property is distributed, either by will or by the laws of descent and distribution.

Successor—One who takes the place of another and continues in their position.

Suicide—The deliberate termination of one's existence.

Surety—A surety is one who undertakes to pay money or perform in the event that the principal fails to do so.

Surrogate—A person appointed to act in place of another.

Survival Statute—A statute that preserves for a decedent's estate a cause of action for infliction of pain and suffering and related damages suffered up to the moment of death.

Taxable Estate—The decedent's gross estate less applicable statutory estate tax deductions, such as charitable deductions.

Tenancy by the Entirety—A form of ownership available only to a husband and wife whereby they each are deemed to hold title to the whole property, with right of survivorship.

Tenancy in Common—An ownership of real estate by two or more persons, each of whom has an undivided fractional interest in the whole property, without any right of survivorship.

Terminal Illness—An incurable condition caused by injury, disease or illness which, regardless of the application of life-sustaining procedures would, within reasonable medical judgment, produce death and where the application of life-sustaining procedures serve only to postpone the moment of death of the patient.

Testate—The state of dying with a valid will in place.

Testator—A male individual who makes and executes a will.

Testatrix—A female individual who makes and executes a will.

Testify—The offering of a statement in a judicial proceeding, under oath and subject to the penalty of perjury.

Testimony—The sworn statement make by a witness in a judicial proceeding.

Title—In property law, denotes ownership and the right to possess real property.

Trust—The transfer of property, real or personal, to the care of a trustee, with the intention that the trustee manage the property on behalf of another person.

Unconscionable—Refers to a bargain so one-sided as to amount to an absence of meaningful choice on the part of one of the parties, together with terms which are unreasonably favorable to the other party.

Unconstitutional—Refers to a statute which conflicts with the United States Constitution rendering it void.

Underwrite—In insurance law, it refers to the assumption of the risk of loss to the insured's person or property, by the insurer of the insurance policy.

Uniform Laws—Laws that have been approved by the Commissioners on Uniform State Laws, and which are proposed to all state legislatures for consideration and adoption.

Usurious Contract—A contract that imposes interest at a rate which exceeds the legally permissible rate.

Usury—An excessive rate of interest above the maximum permissible rate established by the state legislature.

VA Mortgage—A loan guaranteed by the Veterans Administration.

Vested—The right to receive, either at present or in the future, a certain benefit, such as a pension from an employer, without further conditions, such as continued employment.

Visitation—The right of one parent to visit children of the marriage under order of the court.

Vitiate—To make void.

Void—Having no legal force or binding effect.

Void for Vagueness—The term given a criminal statute which is so vague that persons of normal intelligence do not comprehend its application, thus rendering it void.

Voidable—Capable of being rendered void and unenforceable.

Waiver—An intentional and voluntary surrender of a right.

Ward—A person over whom a guardian is appointed to manage his or her affairs.

Will—A legal document which a person executes setting forth their wishes as to the distribution of their property upon death.

Witness—One who testifies to what he has seen, heard, or otherwise observed.

X—Refers to the mark that may be used to denote one's signature when the signer is unable to write his or her name.

BIBLIOGRAPHY

A Guide To Long-Term Care Insurance. Washington, DC: American Association of Retired Persons, 1991.

American Association of Retired Persons (AARP) (Date Visited: April 2001) <http://www.aarp.org/>.

American Bar Association Commission on Legal Problems of the Elderly (Date Visited: April 2001) <http://www.abanet.org/>.

Black's Law Dictionary, Fifth Edition. St. Paul, MN: West Publishing Company, 1979.

Center for Medicare Advocacy (Date Visited: April 2001) <http://www.medicareadvocacy.org/>.

Department of Housing and Urban Development Office of Fair Housing and Equal Opportunity (Date Visited: April 2001) <http://www.fairhousing.org/>.

The Hospice Patient's Alliance (Date Visited: April 2001) <http://www.hospicepatients.org/>.

The Medicare Rights Center (Date Visited: April 2001) <http://www.medicarerights.org/>.

Medicare and You. Baltimore, MD: U.S. Department of Health and Human Services, 1999.

Monthly Vital Statistics Report, Life Expectancy Tables. U.S. Department of Health (Date Visited: April 2001) <http://www.cdc.gov/nchs/>.

National Academy of Elder Law Attorneys (Date Visited: April 2001) <http://www.naela.org/>.

National Senior Citizens Law Center (Date Visited: April 2001) <http://www.nsclc.org/>.

Social Security Administration (Date Visited: April 2001) <http://www.ssa.gov/>.

United States Department of Health and Human Services Office of Disability, Aging and Long-Term Care (Date Visited: April 2001) <http://aspe.os.dhhs.gov/daltcp/home>.